Book of the Hunt

Book of the Hunt

✦

Initiations into the Life of Honor

Tom Dolph

Writers Club Press
New York Lincoln Shanghai

Book of the Hunt
Initiations into the Life of Honor

Writers Club Press
an imprint of iUniverse, Inc.

For information address:
iUniverse, Inc.
2021 Pine Lake Road, Suite 100
Lincoln, NE 68512
www.iuniverse.com

Author's Contact Information:
PO Box 753
Krebs, OK
74554
(918) 423-9329
466-64-3951

ISBN: 0-595-25763-1 (pbk)
ISBN: 0-595-65314-6 (cloth)

Printed in the United States of America

Contents

Introduction

WHO'S GOING TO TELL THE KIDS?

Down Through the ages scholars gazed in wonder at the great pyramids of Egypt. They toiled in vain to discover how the ancients built these great monuments. We still don't know how it was done, and do you know why? Because…someone forgot to tell the kids! It's that simple, all the great questions of history would be answered if only someone had thought to tell the next generation.

Every time an elder dies without passing on his or her unique store of wisdom and experience, a lifetime of wealth is lost to the rest of us.

They say you can't take it with you, but in fact, we succeed in taking our most valuable possession to the grave…our knowledge.

Our present generation has come to believe that any worthwhile knowledge can be reduced to textbook terms or a computer program, and that "old" people have nothing to offer them. They think older people are just "old", used up, out of date, out of touch, out of style and just hanging around waiting to die. In reality, the young are pretty much left to reinvent the wheel for themselves each generation. We leave them a rough sketch and let them figure out the details on their own. But they also need to learn the fine points of coping with life and raising a family, as well as learning the refinements of a craft, trade, art or profession. They need on-the-job-training with the guiding hand of a seasoned veteran, a master of the art, the voice of experience.

America's elders have bought into the idea that they have nothing to offer the younger generation. We have been convinced that the goal of life is to retire, take vacations, have cookouts, join a square dance club, stay "young" and have fun. We should retire, but not to play and not to sit. To retire and return to the irresponsible pursuits of childhood

1

robs us of our status, dignity, purpose and self-esteem. Retire if you like, take a year off and travel, you've earned it; but when you come home, don't sit down…there's work to be done!

Remember what Maggie Kuhn said, "We are the Elders of the tribe. The Elders are charged with the survival and well-being of the tribe."

Western civilization, since the time of the Renaissance and especially since the industrial revolution began, has played out the myth of Faust who sold his soul to the devil for eternal youth, sex, comfort, power and technology. In Goethe's version of the myth, Faust murders an elderly couple for the sole purpose of leveling their cottage so he can have a better view of his domain. Our society worships the false god of "Youth" as did Faust, and it sweeps aside its elders to make room for the sake of immediate convenience.

Society promises "golden years of leisure activity" as a reward for mandatory retirement. It's all propaganda. Insurance statistics show the average life span of retirees is a little more than two years. The cause of death? Lack of purpose in life! Those who beat the statistical odds can expect to be neglected by their children and warehoused in a retirement village or a nursing home. These are little more than concentration camps and prisons to keep elders out of the mainstream of life…mere holding pens for those waiting to die.

Retirement is our greatest opportunity for personal growth and greater contributions to our community and nation. But only so long as we don't accept the "eat, drink, and be merry for tomorrow we die" philosophy.

The idea of a twelve year old out wandering the streets while not knowing how to read or write is an outrage to us; the kid ought to be in school learning! The idea of a seventy-two year old out wandering the streets should be equally appalling. An Elder should be in school too…teaching.

We can reclaim our historic prestige and respect as elders of the tribe, but not by demanding it. We can't demand respect; we have to earn it.

I began this introduction with the above essay in order to justify the writing of this book. This by way of an apology to all the Brothers who may read this and be outraged that someone has had the audacity to set down on paper what has been forbidden for the past eight hundred years.

I do sincerely apologize to those who are offended, but I have received permission from my Elder Brothers to attempt this task. Please remember that we are few and growing fewer every day. We, and our Order, are in very real danger of becoming extinct. Then who will tell the kids? I ask you to remember that the information and wisdom in the following pages has never actually been declared "secret", only PRIVILEGED. I realize there is a certain danger of weakening the effect of the teachings by making them available in print. After many years of concern about this, I've come to see that it also protects it. Scoffers will read and move on. Those who will enter our order will find that knowing certain things in advance has no diminishing effect at all when received personally from their elders. I will elaborate on this topic later on.

To readers in general, I would like to apologize for any lack of literary ability on my part and remind you that this is indeed an important historical and anthropological document. It is the wisdom and knowledge that is of value, not its entertainment potential.

Tom Dolph, LH
McAlester, Oklahoma
August 12, 2000 AD
Orden jahr 809

Part One: A Winter's Tale

THE RAVEN'S APPRENTICE

Once upon a time long ago and far away, there lived a little Prince. He didn't know he was a Prince for the land where he lived was the Land of Trolls. He couldn't remember ever having lived anywhere else, but he knew he didn't feel at home there. He knew no other parents than the Trolls, but felt sure he wasn't truly their son. The trolls were much bigger than the little Prince and were very fierce. Yet, somehow, he sensed the Trolls were just a little frightened by him. Perhaps they were only envious of him, for they didn't always treat him kindly. The Troll parents served him troll food, it tasted nasty and was ugly to look at. When he refused to eat it, the Trolls would become angry and sometimes beat him. Gradually he learned to eat the Trolls' food, but he never learned to like it.

In all fairness, it must be said that the Troll parents seemed to intend no real evil toward the boy; they were just dull, grudging and fearful. Sometimes the little Prince wondered if perhaps they were afraid to do him any real harm. Perhaps he had been left in their care by someone else...perhaps a king, his real father! For while they seemed to care nothing for the boy's upbringing, they were much concerned that he should not be greatly injured or become lost, lest perhaps they should have to answer for their neglect. While he was often beaten, he was seldom marked, often cursed but never cast out.

One day the Prince asked for a drum. "Perhaps", he said, "I will become a drummer boy." Grudgingly the Troll parents agreed and gave him a little drum to play. With the first rat-tat-tat the boy was filled with glee. He beat the drum faster, harder, louder, laughing all the while. Suddenly, the drumhead burst. The drumming stopped, the laughter stopped and the Troll parents were both relieved and angry. They took away the broken drum and hung it high on a wall where the young Prince could see it and be reproached by it but could never reach it again.

"Give me a bow", the little Prince said one day. "For perhaps I will be a Hunter." After much furtive discussion in low tones and with many sidelong glances, the Trolls gave the Prince a little bow and blunted arrows. Again it wasn't long until the Prince drew the bow too far and it broke. And again the Troll parents were angry.

Once the Prince said, "I shall build a little fire in this empty seashell, a brazier for warmth and a lamp for light." The Troll parents smelled the smoke of it and descended upon him howling with wrath. The beating was brutal and long remembered. You see, Trolls have a great fear of fire and light.

"Make me a cape, a hood and a mask", the Prince begged, "for perhaps I shall become a hero and do battle against evil." The Trolls were much amazed. The entire Troll family, with all the uncles and cousins, gathered to discuss it. In the end, they fashioned a cape and cowl, adding even the gauntlets of a knight. But it was all made of paper and much too large for the little Prince. The trolls dressed him in the paper cape amid hoots and howls of giddy delight. Then they each in turn donned the cape and strutted back and forth to gales of laughter. The little Prince never saw the cape again.

Then one day a peddler came and knocked at the door of the Troll house. In his peddler's pack he carried many books. Among these were the Great Books of Places and Things. With much sincere pleading the boy convinced the Troll parents to let him have the Great Books of Places and Things. To be sure, this was an act of uncommon generosity on the part of the Troll parents, and the little Prince came to believe that some power outside of himself had been the true cause in persuading the Trolls to buy the peddler's books for him. This time the Prince was very careful, not a page was torn or smudged, not a cover was scuffed or dented and the Trolls had no cause for complaint, although they did find the books suspicious and worrisome at times. For you see, Trolls have a great superstitious dread of books more so even than of fire. Indeed, to have gained the books had to have been a great and magical event, for from that very day the little Prince's life would change.

He read, and he read, and he read! The books were a mixed blessing however, for he was filled with both great joy and horror by what he learned. The Great books of Places and Things showed him all manner of goodness and evil...some of which he might have hoped to be spared. Splendor and majesty, horror and disgust. He learned more than the books themselves actually spoke, for he had a facile mind, far beyond Troll minds, and saw the greater meanings of things both high and low.

Among these many pleasant and hurtful things he learned of the Great Mountains of the West, far beyond the Land of Trolls. "Perhaps there my kingdom lies," he said to himself, "and when I am grown up, I'll escape the Trolls and wend my way to the high mountains and forests and seek my fortune."

Time passed and the Prince studied hard. He learned all he could about places and things. He learned all the stories the Trolls could tell. He studied the low sorceries and natural magics with which the Trolls ordered their world. There was hardly a subject known to Trolldom that the young Prince had not investigated. He grew wise beyond his years, but was careful to conceal his knowledge for the Trolls would laugh or turn vicious when they thought someone knew more than they.

The Prince hungered to know more than was to be found in books. He yearned with all his heart to learn by experience, to learn with his hands, by touch and habit, to tread the paths of heroes with his own feet, to water his work with his own sweat and see how it grew. But alas, there was no one to teach him. The Trolls were very cautious about letting the Prince handle weapons and tools, nor would they allow him to wander far from sight. No craftsman taught him a trade, no master at arms appeared to show him the ways of a warrior, and no wizard came to teach him enchantments. "Very well," he said, "I shall teach myself!" And so he did. The Prince learned to drive the oxen, to work in wood, stone, clay and metals, the twisting of rope and tying of knots. He taught himself the discerning of pearls and the grading of swine, working in leather and the infusing of herbs.

One day, the half grown Prince encountered a young vagabond Troll along the way near the Troll home. He was actually a runaway, determined to escape his own evil Troll father. Being of about the same age and of like disposition, the Prince and the vagabond became friends of the road and the vagabond told the Prince his tale of woe. Among his meager possessions the runaway carried an old and battered lute. "Tis a poor instrument indeed", he said, "But it plays well enough. I will gladly give it to you in return for a little food. Besides, it is only a burden to me." The Prince was only too happy to make such a fine trade and the vagabond went on his way laden down with a generous store of Troll food.

The Prince soon taught himself to play the weathered old lute, and having reached the limits of its power, he went to the Troll Parents and begged for a newer and better instrument that he might further improve his talents. "Perhaps I shall be a minstrel and a poet", he pleaded. Seeing that The Prince had mastered the lute, the Troll parents reluctantly agreed. "But," they threatened, "see to it that you earn money with your music-making and bring it to us to pay for your keep." Gold was always uppermost in the thoughts of the Troll parents. All Trolls are obsessed by gold. But the Prince was never allowed to go far enough from home to earn the much-wanted gold.

The Prince's greatest pleasure was in making music for himself and the writing of poems, which meant little or nothing to the Trolls. Aside from this, he spent much time trying to teach other young Trolls to play the lute and trying to encourage them to become more than Trolls are accustomed to being. But, sad to say, a Troll is a Troll, and while some learned more than others, too often their only desire was to win fame among their fellow Trolls and to become rich. Such thin soil bore poor harvests.

"Why not become a barber?", complained the Troll father, "Trolls are very hairy and always in need of trimming. It would be a dependable livelihood." "Perhaps you could become a mummer and juggler." Suggested the Troll mother probingly.

"It's quite true, father Troll," said the Prince, "Trolls are much in need of having their hair cut, and while it is an honorable profession, it is not my calling. As for becoming a mummer or juggler, dear mother Troll, I fear it is too frivolous and insincere for me. I am somewhat taciturn and grave of mind. I much prefer solitude. Perhaps I shall pass my days as a hermit."

The Troll parents plotted and schemed, hoping to keep the young Prince within their power while seeming to allow him to grow up and become his own master. It was to little avail, for the Prince was indeed growing up. Soon he was much taller and larger than the Troll parents, and when he looked in the mirror, he saw that he had little in common with them. While it was certain he was born of a Troll mother and father, it was also quite evident that he was not a Troll. No amount of pondering could tell him who he was or what he was meant to be.

"Perhaps I am a Prince in exile. But now that I have reached my full growth, why is it that no messenger has come to call me?"

As you can see, the Prince was now all the more confirmed in his fantasy, the more so for a silent voice began to speak to him. Little by little he grew aware of the voice, which gave him wise counsel and spoke to him of other places and things both far and near; things, which he could not have known by any other means. He began to see the influence of an invisible hand. Perhaps it had always been there, but now its action was clear. While he often failed to understand the ordering and purpose of the unseen hand he came to trust its power, knowing it was always for his eventual good.

Now fully grown, the Prince sought gainful employment as an apprentice in a smithy. Here he worked in iron and brass. Mostly he made tools and implements, which satisfied Trolls, but he secretly taught himself to make ornaments, amulets and talismans of ever-greater beauty and power.

The years passed. The Prince continued to study, to learn, to teach himself what others would not teach him, could not teach him. Never a messenger came from the King; never a master came to guide him. The Prince kept up hope, and yet, from time to time, a little despair crept in.

Then one day a Trickster came to the smithy; a little swarthy man but bright of face and full of mirth. "I've come to work beside you," he announced. "And I wish to be your friend." And so it came to be. The little dark man worked tirelessly, side by side with the Prince, always smiling and in good humor. The swarthy one always had a ready answer for every question and often posed thought provoking questions of his own...questions to which he already seemed to know the answers.

When the day's work was done, the swarthy man would sometimes invite the Prince to walk with him and they would talk. They shared bread together and discussed wide ranging matters, for the dark man had traveled to many far places and knew many dangerous things. However weighty the subject, the dark man always smiled as if knowing something more.

But their friendship was more than walks, talks and breaking bread. As you know, true wisdom comes at the hands of experience. Learning comes with skillful practice, many ordeals and woundings. Many such tests and trials the little man contrived for the Prince. At times these tests seemed mere foolishness and child's play, while some tasks were designed to test the Prince's true mettle. Why so many silly questions and pranks? It seemed beneath the swarthy man's dignity. Only later would the Prince discern their true magical powers to shape and define his destiny.

In time the swarthy man introduced the Prince to his brothers. The Prince found the brothers to be men of noble blood, and the Prince was pleased to be invited to become one with their Brotherhood. And upon a Stone of Honor beneath a great oak tree, deep in the forest, he vowed to share their lot.

The Prince learned much from the brothers, but he found it was only what he himself had already learned from his silent voice. Yet his heart was glad for it confirmed that they were all guided by that same unseen hand. From that day on the Prince strove to speak the truth in all things, to both speak and act in justice and mercy with discretion in all things. He strove to be a good and loyal friend to all just men and boon companion to those whom the brothers favored.

Then one day the swarthy man came to say he must go, "But I will leave you in the care of the Brotherhood." He said. With this the swarthy man departed, never to be seen again.

The winter came and deep gloom settled upon the Prince, and he brooded among the books and relics of his cottage.

One day, as he trudged through the snow clad woods of midwinter, a shiny, black raven suddenly descended upon the path before him. "See me, oh Prince, I am the Raven!" He croaked in raucous tones.

"You call me a Prince? Am I then a Prince indeed?" He asked in astonishment.

"Aye, a Prince and not a Troll at all!" the Raven squawked. "While it is true you were born a son of Trolldom, you have aspired to things good and true and noble."

So, as you already know, the Prince was not really a Prince...not born of royalty...but born of nobility, for nobility is a matter of the heart. We might even say: noble is as noble does.

"I have come to guide you on your quest," the Raven continued, "but I am an impatient guide and will leave you to your own devices unless you follow my lead precisely. Listen well. The man with gold in his hand calls himself rich, but when famine comes there is no bread to buy and he starves. The man with a sundial in his garden looks to the shadow to tell him the hour, but when he is driven from his home he must learn to read the course of the sun itself. Who can say he is an artisan except while he is at his task? Who can say he is a poet except in the midst of composing? Past deeds are no surety of future successes. Only the Man of Honor can stand in honor, proclaiming his calling as the true nature of his soul."

The Raven stamped about in a circle all the while. "Krak, krak, krak", went the Raven, which the Prince took to be Raven laughter.

"See my tracks in the snow?" Asked the Raven. "This is my rune, my signature. Watch for it wherever you go, for where I land, there I leave my mark. The great King of the Universe has sent me to be the guide of the Huntsman, to lead him to game. I always seek the high ground. Remember, Father Noah sent the Raven first to find dry land. Recall that the Ravens fed the Prophet in the desert. I will lead you too upon your quest. But hunt like the wolf, with both speed and stealth, for you also are hunted, pursued by an eight-legged mare whose pace increases with every hoof beat, and whose rider never sleeps nor tires. Where I leave my rune is not a place to camp nor even sleep, do not even halt to rest there. Move on, I point the way. Listen for my song, the Raven's song. Every leaf and tree sings it, every wind and cloud dances to it. My track is my name, it is also the birth rune, the mark of beginnings, the rune of protection, and it is the sign of the oak. Never suffer the woodsman to cut down the Wolf-Tree. For if the Wolf-Tree is felled, I'll have no place to perch. Let them cut the common tree. Let them be fashioned into houses, fences, wheelbarrows and such. The Wolf-Tree is no good for domestic use, it serves far better as the Raven's home. There the Hanged-Man sways in the autumn winds and justice is done. I leave my tracks at every Crossroad to point the way. Be watchful and remember…the Greal you seek is the quest itself, the quest itself is the Greal you seek."

The Prince listened in stunned silence, and then said, "How shall I know this is not a dream? By what token shall I know you?"

At this the Raven pierced his own breast with his long, sharp beak and with the bright drops that melted the snow, the Raven drew the Odal Rune upon the Prince's breast.

"The Odal Rune declares your inheritance, that which is received from your ancestors and held in absolute title, never at the pleasure or whim of any man." The Raven declared. "When you are lost, recall where you came from. Look to your Heart and remember who you are."

And so the Prince set out from his homeland armed with his spear and dagger, tracking the Raven ever westward in search of the Hollow Mountain. "Now," he said to himself, "perhaps I shall find my kingdom!"

But the years passed and he found no homeland, no kingdom. Indeed, he found not so much as the dust on his boots that he could call his own. Everywhere he set foot the Trolls were there before him. It seemed the whole world was enslaved to the power of Trolldom.

He labored in their smithys, he toiled in their scriptoriums, and he served the merchants and moneylenders. He earned his bread at the workbenches of Troll masters wherever he went. From time to time he met others who were of the race of True Men like himself. He spoke to them secretly of the Quest, but most recoiled in fear. So long had they suffered the dominion of Trolls that they no longer dared to dream of freedom. They had become less than Trolls themselves, mere cattle without hope. The Prince spoke before their temples and in their lyceums, he spoke in secret by firelight. He spoke openly and in riddles, but few would listen and fewer still took heart.

Across the seas he traveled to foreign lands. Everywhere the power of Trolldom waxed strong. No kingdom of Honor was to be found. Then, perhaps in despair…he fell ill.

A strange malady consumed him and none could tell its cause. "Perhaps," he said, "it is to a purpose. Surely the Great King will send me aid. Perhaps he will send a great Wizard or Seer to show me the way clearly." But there was only silence and waiting. The impatient Raven flew on and was lost to sight.

Weak and sick unto death he turned homeward. In gloom and despair he made the journey back to the land of his birth. He searched the deepest forests and at last found a quiet cottage. There he vowed to dwell forever, to become a true hermit at last.

Three long years passed and he grew a little stronger. Still no messenger from the King arrived, no track of the Raven was found. All was silence.

From time to time messages of concern came from the brothers of the swarthy man. "Come and stay with us", the messages said, "We will give you bread and companionship. Serve the Quest from our Mountain Fastness." But it was no use. The Prince had not yet learned humility and saw it only as an offer of pity and charity. He would not go to them, but would follow his own course.

In time he grew a little stronger and, as the forest could no longer keep him, he set out for a distant village. He had passed that way before but with never a thought to stop. Now he found it a welcome haven, prosperous and quiet. While the village was under the rule of Trolldom, their power seemed to weigh less heavily than other places.

Another seven years passed. The Prince, while not happy, grew strangely content. He prospered and became well respected. The villagers smiled when they met him and considered it an honor to have him dwell among them. He seldom spoke of the Quest anymore, and then only in riddles. The brothers grew few and far away. The Prince was growing old and comfortable. The Trolls ruled, but the Prince had regained a measure of health and, while he had not found his destiny, he was sure he had found a life.

Then one bright autumn morning, on the occasion of his fiftieth birthday, he stepped out his front door and, to his delight, was instantly greeted by "krak—krak, krak—krak!" Which, as you surely know, means, "Happy birthday, little Prince!" And there above him, perched on the limb of an oak tree, sat the shiny black Raven.

"Thank you, Little Brother! Cried the Prince. "But where have you been? I've waited so long for you!"

"And I've been waiting for you." Answered the Raven.

"But here I am, and here I've been", said the puzzled Prince.

"And here I've been also." Replied the Raven. "The journey of the Quest is not measured in distance alone, but also in time. The years were not complete."

With this the Raven flew away, and for the first time in years the Prince looked up to the sky, the clouds, the tree tops and hills, across the fields and meadows, everywhere he turned he heard the Raven singing, joyously and with great passion. The Prince began to see clearly that the unseen hand had never left him. Every event, every turn of the road had been carefully orchestrated to lead him to this day. Every day the Raven sang and the Prince found the Raven's Rune along every path.

"Tell them!" The Raven sang, "Tell those who will listen. Tell of the Quest, tell of the Great King. Tell them of dragons slain and maidens rescued. Tell them how you defended the honor of the just and show them your wounds and scars. Now they will believe. Write it in a book that those far away may know and join the Brothers of the Hunt. Tell them of the Crusade to be fought. Tell them of the Oak and Stone. And teach them to hear the Raven's Song."

When did I ever accomplish a quest?" The Prince asked in deep dismay. "What dragons have I slain? What maiden did I rescue? How have I defended the just? Upon what Crusade did I ride? My only scars are the wounds of the Initiate, a mere apprentice. The Oak and Stone are far away and none but the Brothers can hear your song."

"Dragons writhe in agony when any True Man stands in Honor." The Raven replied. "Trolls fall back in horror at the sight of noble intent. Demons flee when any temptation is passed by. Justice is upheld with every kind word. Empires of Darkness were conquered with every step you took. Evil is cut down with every thought of beauty. The course of lives have been altered and inspired by your example."

And though the Prince was now old, he began again with renewed heart and determination. He turned with a will to the task of rebuilding the Castles and renewing the Brotherhood.

◆   ◆   ◆

By ones and twos they came. Men began to remember their Heritage. Men were called to Greatness. Men heard the Raven sing. Men saw the banners fly. The news went out far and wide. Men were rising up to cast out the evil of Trolldom. The fires of Chivalry were kindled again from the frost bound shores of Thule to the brazen gates of Samarkand.

And the little Prince, who was not a Prince, but would not be a Troll, lived to see it all. Then, at a good old age, surrounded by the Brothers and all his Grandchildren and kin…he fell asleep.

His ashes rest beneath a great Rune Stone atop a craggy hill, deep in the forest where the wildflowers bloom in the spring and the red and gold leaves gather in autumn. There the birds sing daily, not least among which is heard the Raven's song. And they all lived happily ever after.

Legends of the Hunt

AUDITA TREMENDI

The Third Crusade was proclaimed by Papal Letter on October 29th, in the year of our Lord, 1187. The Emperor Frederick Barbarossa answered that call. History tells us the Emperor died in the East without ever reaching the Holy Land, and that he was buried at Antioch. Legend says he is not dead at all, but that he and his knights sleep in a cave deep in the bowels of a great, high mountain. There the Emperor's flowing red beard, for which he is named, grows ever longer.

From time to time, so the legend goes, Barbarossa's heavy eyelids half open and, lifting a hand, he signals a boy to go forth from the cave to see if the Ravens still fly about the mountain. So long as the Ravens fly he is content to slumber on. But should the day ever come when the boy is sent forth and cannot find the Ravens, then Barbarossa and his knights must arise from their enchanted sleep and ride forth to restore justice and honor to an oppressed and impoverished people.

Scholars tell us, that in an age when even kings were often illiterate, the Emperor Barbarossa was both literate and enlightened. Der Rothbart, as he was called in his own language, encouraged learning among his people and did much to improve their lot in life. The loss of so great a king was almost unbearable to them.

History says that on the tenth day of June in the year of our Lord 1190, Frederick I, called Barbarossa, by the Grace of God, king of the Germans and Emperor of the Holy Roman Empire, drowned while crossing the river Salef in Armenia.

In the autumn of that same year, the Teutonic Order was founded at Acre in the Holy Land. The order first consisted of monks dedicated to the care of the sick and wounded, just as medical corpsmen care for the war wounded in a modern army.

In November of 1198, a second branch was formed at Acre, The Order of Teutonic Knights. Part of the avowed mission of these warrior monks was to establish and defend civilized Christian culture among the pagans. The most famous of its grand masters was Hermann of Salza, to whose wisdom and piety popes and emperors united to do honor. The Teutonic knights are less celebrated for their deeds in the Holy Land than for their service in civilizing the wild tribes along the Baltic, whither they retired when they returned from Palestine. Under their care churches were founded, fields were cleared and converted to farms, and the whole face of northern Europe was changed.

As with other orders of chivalry, such as the Knights Templar and the Hospitalers, the Teutonic Order had a third branch consisting of men at arms. The fourth branch consisted of servants, stewards, clerks, cooks and the like. All of these were sworn to the same vows as their lords, and were often more dedicated to those vows than were their high-born masters.

Seldom mentioned directly, but often alluded to, were the Huntsmen, a fifth branch of the order. While monks were normally forbidden to eat meat, the Pope, because of the active nature of the knights' vocation, permitted them to eat meat, but as with all other monks, they were forbidden to personally hunt game. We see then the need to enlist a band of Huntsmen, but they served in a further capacity, especially once they returned to northern Europe and the Crusade against the pagans of the East.

The Emperor Barbarossa had long since dubbed his wily, battle-wise foot soldiers "War Ravens", after their common practice of returning to the battlefield to strip the enemy dead of weapons and gear. This, of course, was a large part of their wages. The Huntsmen, who served as scouts, spies, couriers and assassins, also had a part in looting the dead, but their claim to the title of Ravens had already been established in the dim mists of antiquity.

These Ravens, these Huntsmen, this fifth branch of the order, these are our fraternal ancestors. They too had formalized themselves into a guild, an order within the order. Drawing on the myths and teachings of their pagan ancestors, they formed a distinct Brotherhood known by many names, but formally called, Orden der Valknut, and the Order of the Death bond.

The Valknut trained both knights and foot soldiers in the methods of guerilla warfare in the forests of the East. These Ravens of the Hunt continued to serve the Order loyally, but as the centuries slipped by the Teutonic Knights sank into corruption and greed. The knights became little more than merchant princes and power brokers; robber barons, politicians, lords of commerce and oath breakers. Still, for the sake of their vow, the Ravens remained loyal to the Teutonic Order.

The last Grand Master of the Teutonic Knights was the Emperor of Austria. He assumed the mantle in 1805. Napoleon Bonaparte dissolved the order the following year. Now, at last, the Ravens were free. In that year of 1806 the Order of the Valknut declared its independence from the Teutonic Order.

In 1840, the Austrian Empire again set up the order of Teutonic Knights, but the true line of succession had been broken and no Grand Master could reclaim authority over the Brothers of the Valknut.

In 1820, a young man of Irish-English descent named Kenelm Digby was initiated into the Brotherhood at the ruined castle of Ehrenbreitstein in Germany. In time he wrote a book entitled, "The Broad stone of Honor". This book, which eventually grew into four volumes and a fifth, was a celebration of the medieval code of chivalry. While Sir Walter Scott inspired the rebirth of chivalry in Victorian England and America, it was the works of Digby, which instructed them in its application. While Digby was careful to never mention the order of the Valknut or its traditions in writing, he made use of the order's teachings and dropped numerous hints that would identify him to others of the order. The very title of the book itself is the first clue.

Many great names have been enrolled in our order; Robert Louis Stevenson, George Eastman and John Steinbeck among others. While never large, the order has steadily declined over the past century or so. While our ranks have thinned, the Ravens still fly...and Barbarossa slumbers on.

Traditions of the Hunt

THE MAKING OF THE HUNTSMAN

In ancient times, **the First Initiation** took place when a boy was seven years old. Today this is seldom the case; it usually happens thus only within families which hold the Traditions of the Valknut. Most now enter the Order as adolescents or grown men, still they must undertake the first initiation. This is no disgrace.

At some point, after the apprentice has spent enough time with his Anwalt, his mentor, he will be instructed to gather a small bundle of dry sticks and tinder and to steal the wooden spoon from his mother with which he was fed as a child, or to take the whorl with which his mother spun thread or yarn to make his clothes. In this 21st century it is usual to ask instead for a photograph of the initiate's mother as wooden spoons and whorls are in short supply. In addition the initiate is told to bring his favorite childhood toy or a reasonable facsimile thereof. He will also be expected to bring flint and steel.

Sometime following the autumnal equinox and the first frost of autumn, the initiate receives word that, "The Sackman is coming for you." He must have all the above named items gathered together and ready to depart. The initiate is expected to be standing at his door waiting when the Sackman arrives. The Sackman will indeed be carrying a sack and will escort the initiate to a remote wooded area out of sight and sound or any hint of civilization. At some convenient place, the Anwalt will stop and tell the initiate to dig a hole in the trail. Sitting crouched across from the initiate, the Anwalt will indicate the item belonging to the initiate's mother and ask him what it is. The initiate will answer. The Anwalt will then say, "Bury it!" In the case of a photograph, it must be placed face down in the hole so as not to throw dirt in her face; you are burying your mother, no insulting her. The initiate must then scatter a handful of dirt on the item. The Anwalt will then indicate the toy and ask, "What is that?" The initiate answers, "It is the toy of my childhood." "Bury it!" the Sackman will say. The toy is then placed in the same hole and a handful of dirt is scattered over it. The Sackman will then ask, "Do you do this willingly?" The initiate must answer, "With all my heart and no regrets." The Anwalt then grabs the initiate by the upper right arm firmly and gruffly says, "Be thou henceforth a man forever!"

"Finish it." The Sackman instructs. When the hole is filled and tamped down, the Sackman arises and blindfolds the initiate. The Anwalt places the initiate's right hand on the Anwalt's left shoulder and leads him further down the trail out of sight of the place where the past was buried. In the case of a seven year old child, the Anwalt takes the boy's right hand in his left hand and leads him home again. This is the first initiation.

The Second Initiation is conducted when the boy is fourteen years old, as always, after the autumnal equinox and following first frost. In the initiation of adult males, the first and second initiations may be combined. (Please note: if the initiate is only seven years old and no second initiation is to be performed, the bundle of sticks and fire-making implements are not required, only the toy and the item representing the initiate's mother are needed.) In this the initiate is led blindfolded further down the trail to a clearing on the edge of the woods where the ground is clean and even. Here the blindfold is removed and the initiate is given a peg of wood, bone or antler with a length of cord about the height of a man attached to it. The other end is attached to the base of the Anwalt's walking staff. The initiate is instructed to drive the peg into the ground and describe a circle with the staff. The initiate remains inside the circle as he marks it out upon the ground.

The initiate is then instructed to sit down in the center of the circle. The Anwalt then walks slowly around the outer perimeter of the circle in a clockwise fashion while speaking to the initiate. "This is you. This is your world. This is your little self. It is nothing but a circle in the dirt. It is cold, damp, dirty and useless. And there you sit in the middle, the king of dirt, the king of nothing! Get up and build a fire."

The initiate then takes the little bundle of sticks, tinder, flint, and steel, and strikes a fire in the center of the circle. The Anwalt sits down on the ground to the north of the circle and watches. The Anwalt directs the initiate to sit down with his back to the fire facing his mentor. Since the initiation begins at sunset (although this is not always the case, it can also be conducted at midday), the fire may already cast a shadow. The Anwalt will draw the initiate's attention to his shadow cast before him by the fire and instruct him in this manner:

"Now your world is a bit warmer, but you can no longer be the center of your little kingdom, you would be consumed by the fire. You must ever move around the center. You must tend the fire to maintain the light and warmth. You must ever tend the flame in order to reap the benefits of light, warmth and protection from the demons of night. And yet, wherever you sit, a shadow remains in the circle with you. The shadow is attached to you and is ever with you. The flame doesn't create the shadow, you do. Only if you stood in the midst of the fire would the shadow vanish, but you would be consumed by the fire. You have the power of the fire, but you are not the fire."

"I have more than words for you, but I cannot give it to you at so great a distance. May I enter and sit with you?"

The initiate answers, "Please, come in and sit with me."

The Anwalt rises and is given the peg and cord. He then drives the peg into the ground some distance to the north of the initiate's circle and with his staff describes an arc which cuts across the initiate's circle and creates a space known as a mandorla. The Anwalt does not draw a complete circle, but leaves the arc open to the whole of creation. The mandorla is large enough to seat both the Anwalt and his initiate. The

Anwalt then asks the initiate to be seated in the west end of the man-dorla. The Anwalt sits cross legged in the east end facing the initiate.

The Anwalt then asks the initiate, "Do you want to live or do you want to die?" The initiate answers, "I want to live."

"As a man of honor?" the Anwalt asks.

"As a man of honor. I would be your Brother." The initiate replies.

"Then I must first be to you an uncle." Responds the Anwalt.

Here the Anwalt takes a small bag of dust, which he has gathered from a crossroad, and with it draws a small cross on the ground between them. He then says, "The decision is made, a new course is set. For a thing to live, something must die. It is the Law."

The Anwalt then draws a dagger from the sack (this is a dagger which the Anwalt has previously loaned to the initiate at an earlier time in the initiate's training. He was instructed to return it as soon as possi-ble with a razor sharp point and edge. The Anwalt then tied it with a peace bond and put it away for this very occasion.) The Anwalt lifts the dagger and holds it to catch the fire light. Slowly turning the blade, he recites, "Behold the dagger and runes I make. Behold the blade honed for my blood's sake."

Here the Anwalt opens his shirt and pierces his own left chest over the heart. With the blade of the dagger he scoops up the blood, instructs the initiate to open his own shirt, and with the bloodied blade draws the odal rune upon the initiate's left chest. Again he recites a verse, "My blood will die and yet it lives, in ages to come for the life it gives."

The mentor then presses a clean white folded cloth against the ini-tiate's chest to soak up some of the blood rune as a lasting reminder of the day. The Anwalt then binds his own wound and says yet another verse as he wipes the dagger clean and turns it in the fire light.

"Watch and see the sheen and shade as the Raven perches and turns on the Dagger's blade. Never can I turn its edge to thee that its edge is not turned as well toward me. I send you turning like an oak leaf in the winter wind, return with honor that my wound may mend."

The Anwalt then gathers a handful of cedar chips from his sack and places them on the fire. He then takes a burning stick from the fire, puts out its flame and lays it on the ground to cool while he prepares for the next part of the rite.

The Anwalt produces a drinking gourd, which he places on the ground between them. Into the gourd he drops a small stone engraved with an odal rune and fills the gourd with water from a jar. Then he says,

"The fire you tend reveals your griefs." He then takes up the charred stick and smears its ashes on the initiate's right palm saying, "This is your guilt." He smears ashes on the initiate's right cheek saying, "This is your shame."

He smears the initiate's left cheek saying, "This is injustice in the world."

He smears the initiate's left palm saying, "This is the straw death."

Finally, he bids the initiate to put out his tongue and this smears ashes on it saying, "This is the desire of your heart."

Again the mentor smears the initiate's right palm, forming a cross as he says, "The guilt is what you have done. For this you deserve to die."

Completing the cross on the initiate's right cheek he says, "The shame is what you are. For this you deserve pity."

Smearing the left cheek again, he says, "Injustice is the way of the world."

Smearing his left palm again, he says, "The straw death is the death without purpose."

And again smearing the initiate's tongue, he says, "The desire of your heart is withheld from you."

Here the mentor takes up the gourd and pours a little clean water on a clean white cloth and wipes the right hand twice, saying, "We share your guilt, but God forgives guilt."

Wiping the right cheek twice, he says, "We too feel shame, but God takes away shame." Wiping the left cheek twice, he says, "We stand with you against injustice. God will punish the unjust."

Wiping the left hand twice, he says, "May God bless your endeavor as we honor your martyrdom."

The Anwalt then hands the gourd to the initiate and bids him to rinse his mouth with the water and spit the water outside the circle. The Anwalt then pours a small amount of mead into the remaining water in the gourd and gives it to the initiate instructing him to take a drink. The Anwalt then takes the gourd and says,

"May God grant you the desire of your heart as surely as we are your companions on the quest." The Anwalt then drinks the last of the water and mead himself.

The mentor then gives a smooth stone to the initiate saying,

"We honor your quest and extend to you the favor and protection of the Brotherhood of the Sicarii, Order of the Valknut; to you and your house."

(Favor and protection are conferred upon the initiate himself, all female relatives, male relatives under the age of fourteen or over the age of fifty, and to all his property.)

With this, the mentor silently gathers his instruments back into his sack, leaves the circle and walks down the trail some distance where he waits while the initiate says his prayers and spends a few minutes contemplating the stone and the day's events. The initiate then puts out the fire, scatters the circle, and gathers up the stone and the cloth bearing his Anwalt's blood rune and returns back down the trail to join his mentor.

It is customary for the initiate and his teacher to share a meal that evening. During this time, the Anwalt will instruct the initiate in "The Hanged Man's Repose". This is a position assumed immediately after retiring to bed each night. The Hanged Man consists of drawing the right ankle up and placing it behind the left knee while lying on one's back. The right hand is placed over the heart, the left hand is placed on top of the right hand and the pads of the thumbs are placed against each other. The Old Brothers believed this position brought wisdom and good health. It also stands as a reminder of one's pledge and purpose as a Brother. It isn't necessary to sleep in this position, but only to assume the Hanged Man's pose for a few moments prior to sleep.

TENDING THE FIRE. This is the next step in the initiation process. The initiate is now a questor, a hunter, and some time between his second and third initiation procedure he must undergo a three day sojourn in the wilderness alone. He is instructed in how this is to be carried out and is left to the undertaking on his own recognizance.

The questor is to return to the woods and select a place where he will not be disturbed for three full days. The site should, ideally, be located just at the edge of a clearing in the woods. The questor will need to provide himself with an ample supply of drinking water and fire wood as he isn't permitted to leave the fire for the entire period. His vigil should begin shortly before sunset. He must again draw a circle with the additional arc creating the mandorla (also known as a PENUMBRA). The penumbra serves as his doorway into and out of the circle. He must enter and exit only through the penumbra. Once he has built the fire, he must not leave the circle until sundown three days later. The questor can bring a sleeping bag, additional clothing, toilet paper, a spade for digging his in-circle latrine, matches and/or flint and steel, a journal and pen, plus any weapons he wishes. He will of course, also have brought a walking staff, cord and peg to inscribe the circle. Finally, he will have brought the smooth stone presented to him by his mentor. This is called a kinstone (or kenstone, or soul stone).

No food is permitted inside the circle. This is to be a three day total fast. In the event of an emergency, or if the questor must make a long trek to and from the site, he may bring enough food for one meal and leave it outside the circle until he leaves. He may take only water during this time. His sole purpose in being here is to tend the fire, pray, contemplate his life and eventual death, his purpose in this life, and to record any insights or thoughts he may wish in his journal. The only deviation from this regimen is the brief daily exercise of "Shadow Casting".

Each day, when the sun is at its zenith, he must place the kinstone in the center of the mandorla, step back, raise his hands in the sign of the Raven so that the Raven's shadow falls on the stone, then repeats this prayer: "Oh Lord God, Creator of the universe and all that dwells therein/I beseech Your pity for my life of sin/as the Raven overshadows and darkens the stone/so my soul is burdened as I watch here alone/release from my heart the demons of old/fill them with light and turn them to gold/warm this stone of my soul/give it wisdom and grace/that I may serve Thee with honor til we meet face to face/in the name of your Son and the Holy Spirit I pray/till the Morning Star rises and brings the New Day. Amen."

As the sun sets on the third day, the questor is free to bury the fire, clear the site and return home.

Sometime prior to his third initiation, the questor should carve the kinstone with his family name and a rune of his choice. A common choice is the Odal rune which symbolizes "heritage", that which we receive from our forefathers, that which is ours by right, and not at the pleasure or whim of any man.

The Third Initiation is granted at the age of twenty one, providing the Elder Brothers deem the questor worthy of this great honor. This event brings the questor to full manhood and into equal fellowship of the Brotherhood. Here he becomes a true Huntsman. This is the VALKNUT, the Death Bond. This rite, by means of the principle of mystical contagion, is our direct link to our ancestors and the traditions of the Old Brothers. This is the bond between those who died with honor and those who live in honor.

The rite of the Death Bond is always held in a deep forest or atop a craggy hill, a "tor", far removed from sight, sound or any hint of civilization. There is this exception: The rite may also be conducted on an ancient battle site, at or within sight of a ruined fortress, or other ancient and revered ruin, so long as no other work of man intrudes.

A fully matured oak tree is the focus of this rite; preferably the oldest and largest in the vicinity. If possible a "wolf tree" should be chosen.

A Cross or the Antioch Banner is then hung on the west side of the tree trunk. The Altmann, the oldest man in the troop, will stand before this, facing west during the rite. In front of the Altmann stands a tree stump about four feet high. On this pediment an Honor Stone is placed. A small rush lamp filled with olive oil is placed on one corner of the stone. A few feet further to the west, a flat hearth stone is laid. Ideally, if there are enough old men in the troop, four more stumps are placed in line with the oak tree; two to the north, two to the south. Here the Elders will sit during the rite. Surrounding all of this are five smooth, rounded stones; one to the north, one to the east, one to the south and two to the west marking the entry point to the symbolically described circle.

At the appointed time, following the autumnal equinox and first frost, preferably on the eve of the Feast of Saint Hubert of Liege, patron saint of Huntsmen (November third), the old men arrive before sunset to clear and arrange the site.

At sunset, the Elders take their seats to the left and right of the oak tree. The Altmann then enters, places his right hand on the stone, touches his left chest and salutes the Cross or Banner, steps around behind the stone and faces the west. Those Brothers of the Order who are in attendance to witness the event, then enter and form a semicircle in the northwest and southwest quadrants of the circle on either side of the entry stones.

The Anwalt then steps into the circle and stands to the south of the hearth stone and faces north. He is joined on the north side of the stone by the next senior Brother of the Order who stands facing south. If no other Brother is present, the Anwalt will call his apprentice (the questor to be initiated) into the circle to stand this position. The senior

Brother or the questor then assists the Anwalt in kindling a fire on the hearth stone using flint and steel.

When the flame is lighted and sure, the Anwalt will lift a burning brand and carry it to the Honor Stone where he will light the rush lamp. The Anwalt then steps back, calls "Salute!" and all raise their hands to the Antioch Banner. The Anwalt then returns to his position south of the Hearth stone.

The questors, having been led blindfolded in single file, wait just outside the entry stones. They are each accompanied by their respective sponsors (also known as Anwalten; counselors).

The Altmann raises his hands and speaks the invocation: LORD GOD, CREATOR OF THE UNIVERSE AND ALL THAT DWELLS THEREIN, WE BESEECH THEE IN THE NAME OF YOUR ONLY BEGOTTEN SON, JESUS CHRIST, BY THE POWER OF THE HOLY SPIRIT, TO LOOK UPON THIS GATHERING WITH FAVOR. LET OUR RITES BE HAL-LOWED BY YOUR PRESENCE AND MAKE YOUR PURPOSE OUR PURPOSE. AMEN.

The Altmann takes up the Spear and says, "Bring forth the questors."

Each questor is brought into the circle led by his sponsor who then stands to the north of the heart stone while the Anwalt remains stand-ing to the south. Each questor is brought in one at a time to complete the initiation. The Anwalt (or the Altmann, if the initiation party is small) then challenges the sponsor by asking, "Has this questor been counseled and tested in accordance with the rule of our Order?"

The sponsor replies, "He has, Sir. Permit him to take the vow of Honor."

The Anwalt (or Altmann) then says, "So be it!" Here the sponsor raises the questor's blindfold from the questor's left eye only, and says, "Behold the Banner of Christ, the Stone of Honor, the spear of Mar-tyrdom and the Brothers of the Oak and Stone."

The questor is led forward to the Honor Stone by the Anwalt where the Altmann asks, "Do you submit willingly and with true conscience to the rule of this Order, and to the duties of Manhood?" The questor answers, "I do, by the Grace of God."

The Altman passes the point of the Spear through the flame of the lamp saying, "Then pledge your word in blood." And extends the spear toward the questor.

The questor must grasp the spear's socket and stab himself in the left chest. The questor then takes the blood from the wound with the fingers of his right hand, lays it upon the Honor Stone and says, "I pledge my life, loyalty and fortune to the Cause of Christ our Saviour, and vow to uphold and defend with my life's blood, the honor, ideals and purposes of the Brotherhood of the Sicarii, Order of the Valknut. By the Grace of God Almighty, through the power of the Holy Spirit. Amen." The questor salutes the Banner, steps back one pace and turns to face the Anwalt who stands directly behind him.

The Anwalt draws his dagger and lays it on the questor's left shoulder. At the same time, the Altmann extends the Spear and rests its blade on the questor's right shoulder. The Anwalt then says, "In recognition of your devotion to the Cause of Christ, our common heritage and purpose, we do henceforth and forever esteem you as a Man of Honor, and worthy of the name. We welcome you as a Brother."

The dagger and spear are withdrawn and the Anwalt returns to his post, next to the hearth stone. The four elders step forward to bestow the tokens of the Order. (In the absence of elders, any one or more of those present, including the Altmann and Anwalt, may bestow the tokens).

The first token is a piece of flint. The second token is a rune stave made of oak. The third token is a cup of cold water. The fourth token is the dagger used by the questor's sponsor to bestow the blood rune in the second initiation.

The new Brother turns again to the Altmann, salutes and steps back as the Altmann returns the salute saying, "Depart in Honor, live in Honor, die in Honor,"

The new Brother turns to the south and, accompanied by his sponsor, steps to the end of the semi-circle where his wound is dressed. Both men then take their places as equals in the circle. Meanwhile, the next questor is called forward and the ritual is repeated.

When all new Brothers have completed their initiation, the Altmann calls, "Are there bright daggers among you? Bring them forth." Those who have just received their new daggers, and those who have acquired new daggers from whatever source since the last Valknut ceremony, step forward together. They lift their daggers in a salute so that all the blades touch each other. The Altmann extends the spear to touch the blades and pronounces the Consecration of Arms: HEARKEN WE BESEECH THEE, O LORD, TO OUR PRAYERS, AND DEIGN TO BLESS WITH THE RIGHT HAND OF THY MAJESTY THESE DAGGERS, THAT THY SERVANTS MAY BE ARMED IN DEFENCE OF THE FAITH; PRESERVERS OF ALL THAT IS NOBLE, PROTECTORS OF THE FAITHFUL, A SCOURGE TO PAGANS, A TERROR AND DREAD TO THE WICKED, THAT THEY MAY BE HONORABLE AND JUST IN BOTH ATTACK AND DEFENCE. AMEN. The Brothers say, "Amen!" and return to their ranks.

The Altmann then says, "Let us concur in the bonds of Brotherhood." At this, the Anwalt steps forward, touches the Honor Stone with his right hand, strikes his left chest with his right hand clenched, then opens his hand and raises it in salute to the Antioch Banner (or Cross). He then steps to the south end of the circle. The senior Huntsman then steps forward, repeats the salute and steps to the north end of the circle. Those center of the semi-circle advance, each in turn, one from the left, then from the right, to salute in like manner, exiting one to the left, the next to the right. When the last Brother has saluted and returned to the circle, the Elders come forward to stand before the

Stone and salute together. Finally, the Altmann steps to the front of the Stone, salutes and then turns to the assembled Brothers and delivers the closing Benediction: DEPART IN THE PEACE OF GOD. AMEN.

The Anwalt and the senior Huntsman begin the Hymn of the Brotherhood as they turn to leave the circle. The entire gathering joins the singing and follows to exit the circle. The Altmann follows last, leaving the Elders to quench the fire and lamp, remove the Honor Stone and Banner (or Cross) and to clear the site.

NOTE: In the event that no initiations are to take place, the observance of the Valknut rite proceeds directly from the Invocation to the dedication of new daggers.

New Brothers are escorted directly to a comfortable place to share a meal with their Counselors. Following this, the new Brothers are taught the **Four Truths and the Fifth Truth**. These are, first: YOU MAY SERVE THE KING, BUT YOU MUST NEVER BE THE KING'S MAN. The Second is this: YOU ARE THE DAGGER, THE DAGGER IS THE HUNT, THE HUNT IS HONOR, HONOR IS MERCY. The third Truth is this: THE HUNTER AND THE RAVEN WILL FIGHT AGAINST THE ANTICHRIST; WE ARE THE BANDS OF ORION. The Fourth Truth is: GOD GIVES US THE POWER OF LAUGHTER, THE RAVEN GIVES US CAUSE TO LAUGH. And the Fifth: EVERY TIME YOU FART, SAY, "LIFE IS GOOD!"

The Fourth Initiation is called THE RAVEN'S REST. As always, it is conducted in the fall. Autumn is the season of Men. Of Old Men. The time of harvest. Full of growth and wisdom. The time when the world's work is done. The season of growing slows. Halts. The season when seed pods are heavy with experience and skill, and turn back to the earth. A time to reap what has been sown. A time for winnowing the harvest. Separating the good. Burning the chaff for heat and light. The straw spreads out to cover the earth. To protect it from the winter winds. The fruit is divided among the little ones. The children are nourished. The animals are fed. The land is replenished. The flowers, long since brittle and dry. The time for wandering has come. The Hunt without prey. A time of grief, not of death to come, but for growing not done—and for growing done. Grief turns to wisdom. Wisdom turns to joy. Release from the demands of war and the Hunt. The bow is cast aside gladly. His was the freedom to choose. But freedom from the need to choose is freedom indeed. It's time to eat the Raven's bread. To evoke the Changer. The reconciler of opposites. The Lord of irony. The Guardian of wintry fields. Time to rest and take one's turn as the Teller of winter's tales.

And so he comes. This Huntsman of fifty autumns. This veteran of fifty campaigns. An acorn tight in his fist. He bestows it on a younger Brother. One he himself has sent turning in the world. "Now it's time for the Raven's Rest." He says. The words don't come hard or grudgingly. They come sad and beautiful and welcome, like the memories of youth.

The children run laughing to the woods. Gathering acorns. Mothers and young women follow. Baskets in hand. Young men. Armed. Stand guard.

Bad acorns, like witches, float in water and are cast away. Old women crush the acorns. Leach out the bitterness. Wash it away. They bake the Raven's Bread. Every hand touches it. A blessing in which all have a part.

The old Hunter returns to the killing field. He sits in silence. He calls up past victories. He looks to the mountains of the West. He waits. The Brothers come. Their women come. The children come. They sit down before him. He that received the acorn uncovers the bread. "We are honored to bring you this loaf as duty commands." The old man accepts the Bread saying, "This is the Bread of the Oak. The Bread of Honor. The Bread of the Sicarii. The Bread of the Huntsman. The Raven's Bread. Never to be shared with an unbeliever. Never to be eaten under a roof, or without a blessing. Today I lay aside the tatstock and bow. I pass the Raven's Bread to you. Whole and unbroken, as I received it from my Elders."

The younger Huntsman breaks the Bread. Entices the old man with a morsel. "Stay yet awhile, Grey Man. Eat with us. Share with us your wisdom. Teach our sons to tend the fire. To stone the blade. To master the Runes."

The old man touches the morsel to the broken loaf. He blesses it. He tastes the morsel. "This bread is good." He replies. The Huntsman no-more clasps hands with the Elder not-yet. The pledge is sealed. The Grey Man scatters the last of his portion of Bread as crumbs for the birds. A token of his care and stewardship of all living.

The young Huntsmen. Arms at the ready. Lead the way back to fireside and feast. The Elders and the New Elder follow. The women follow. The children follow. The Raven has come to rest.

The Raven's Bread is eaten and scattered along the way. The wilderness rejoices.

And there is the FIFTH INITIATION…which I do not recommend. In truth, there is almost nothing I can tell you about it. I have not undergone this observance, nor do I know anyone who has. My sponsor is dead. My mentor is gone away, and for reasons I would rather not discuss, I'm reluctant to seek him out and impose upon him for greater insight. This much I can tell you; it is called the Hanged Man. It can be conducted for anyone who has undergone the Third Initiation, at any time he chooses. When anyone asks about the Fifth Initiation, or anytime it is mentioned, the Elder is required to say, "I do not recommend it." The Elder is required to give this same reply three times. If the same Brother asks a fourth time, the Elder will again reply, "I do not recommend it." But he will then discuss it to whatever degree the questioner requires. This is what I know:

The Initiate is taken to the woods; there a stout rope is thrown over a branch of a large Oak tree and made fast. The Initiate has a thick padding of fur, sheep skin or a blanket wrapped around his left ankle, and the rope is tied securely around this; tight enough to hold his weight, but not so tight as to cut off the flow of blood to his foot. His wrists are bound behind his back, again loosely; more I think to keep his hands in position than to prevent escape. He is then hoisted upside down by the rope so that his head is only a few inches off the ground. A long pole is pushed between the strands of the rope and the opposite end of the pole is left to rest on the ground. This serves to adjust the Initiate's position. As the rope stretches, the Initiate's body will begin to turn this way or that. The pole can be moved to keep the Initiate always facing west. Two small fires are built, one to the north and one to the south of the Initiate. The south fire is allowed to burn itself out, the north fire must be continually fed for the next three days. A Watcher remains with the Initiate to feed the fire. He must sit a good distance from the Initiate except for the times he approaches to feed the fire. He is never to speak to the Hanged Man. The Hanged Man is to have no water or food during this entire three days. At the end of three days (or sooner, if the Hanged Man demands it), he is cut down, given food and water and tended as he is very likely to need care.

What words are said to him or in his presence before or after the observance, I do not know…if indeed anything is said. What prayers the Hanged Man is to say, if any, I don't know. What he is to think or how he is to direct his mind, I do not know. I am told this much, one of four things may happen. First, he may die. Secondly, he may go mad. Thirdly, he may be crippled. Fourthly, he may gain miraculous powers of prophecy, powers of healing and miraculous abilities. And a fifth, nothing at all may happen.

Obviously, the Fifth Initiation is optional. It is neither required nor recommended. Only those who feel led to undertake it should risk it.

The DENKMAL. This is a very important exercise. I believe it is a recapitulation of the Four Initiations and the Fifth. The Denkmal should be performed often; everyday, once a week, or as often as is possible. I believe it reinforces the teachings, principles and ceremonies that the Huntsman has been granted. It is complicated and difficult to describe. To aid the student in learning this exercise see the pages of illustrations at the end of the book. The instructions are as follows.

The Denkmal may be done under a roof or in the open air. Be careful to choose a direction that seems best for you and always face that direction wherever you perform the exercise. Sit flat on the ground with the left leg extended more or less straight out in front of you. The right leg should be drawn up with the right ankle beneath the left knee. Lay your initiation dagger on the ground in front of you with the point facing straight ahead. Be sure the dagger is laying so that the Odal Rune carved on the haft faces up and is visible.

Quiet the mind for a moment, then lift both hands, palms flat with the thumbs pointed out at right angles and touching each other. Gaze momentarily at the dagger between your hands. Then lean the hands toward each other until the index finger tips touch forming a triangle while still gazing at the dagger through the triangle formed by the hands. Rotate the right hand downward, around and up behind the left hand so the palm of the right hand now faces you. At the same time, turn the left hand to the right so that the left palm also faces you. The tips of the thumbs should continue to touch throughout this movement. In this position, momentarily gaze at the dagger over the tips of the thumbs. Maintaining this position, bring the hands back and press them against your chest over the heart. Then move the left hand to the left knee while reaching with the right hand, grasp the dagger with the right hand, bring it up and lightly strike the left chest with the flat of the blade. Turn the handle of the dagger in your hand and strike the left chest with the other side of the blade. Turn the handle yet again and strike the chest a third time with the opposite side of the blade. Turn the handle a fourth time and strike the chest with the flat of the blade. Then take the dagger in your left hand and lay the flat of the blade across the right eye and hold it for a moment. Now lean forward and replace the dagger on the ground in front of you with the blade pointed to your right and return your hands crossed, left over right, with the pads of the thumbs touching, to your heart.

Gather your thoughts, stay focused on what you're doing, then return the left hand to the left knee, while reaching for the dagger with the right hand. Lift the dagger, kiss the flat of the blade and lift it high and somewhat to your right while gazing at the blade. Hold this position for a moment and immediately return the dagger to the ground with the blade pointed toward you. Return your hands to your chest, left over right as before.

Collect your thoughts, then with the left hand, grasp the dagger and holding it horizontally with the edge turned toward you at eye level, gaze at the edge of the blade. You will be holding the dagger in your fist with the blade pointed to your left. You will be gazing across your forearm at the edge of the blade. Hold it in this position for a moment, then bring your left hand around toward your right shoulder where you will rest the palm of your right hand on the pommel with the blade now pointed straight ahead of you. Hold this position for a moment then thrust straight ahead at arm's length, as if stabbing someone. Hold the position for a moment then quickly return the dagger to the ground. The blade will now be pointed to your left. Return your hands to the crossed position on your chest.

Focus on the fourth pass. When you are ready, drop the left hand to the left knee while grasping the dagger and raising it so that the blade is pointed upwards with the flat of the blade turned toward you. Steady your position by grasping the dagger with both hands now.

Fix your gaze steadily on or slightly above the very tip of the point. Hold this position for as long as you like (usually two or three minutes). It is best if the background is somewhat dark. Within several seconds you will see a tiny thread of pure light streaming upward from the point of the blade. At other times, you may see two curved streams of light arcing upward from the blade in exactly the shape of the blade, like a mirror image of the blade's outline. Then return the dagger to the ground and place your hands on your chest again.

The final pass consists of placing the first three fingers of the left hand on the handle of the dagger which now points away from you, as if to steady it. Then, lift the right hand with the first two fingers pointed upward and the third and fourth fingers folded into the palm and the thumb folded over touching the third finger. Hold this pose for a moment, then bring the hand down quickly laying the two fingers along the blade of the dagger. Hold this pose for a moment, then quickly pick up the dagger with your right hand and lay it aside. The Denkmal is completed.

You should immediately get up, move around, do something else. Eat something, drink something, wash your face, anything that will help to break the mindset and distance you from the exercise you have just completed.

It will take a certain amount of practice to learn to perform the Denkmal in a smooth and orderly fashion. When you are practicing this exercise and make a mistake, stop, take the dagger in your left hand and knock on the blade with the knuckles of your right hand four times. Turn the dagger over and rap on the other side once. Then begin at the beginning and do the entire exercise over again until you have mastered it.

The RUNA. The Brothers gather for a meeting once a week. Whatever day of the week a particular Hunt chooses. This meeting is called a Runa, which means a "secret gathering". The Runa should last about three hours, usually in the evening. Those permitted to attend include all members of the Hunt, their apprentices and any prospective recruits. Care should be given not to discuss matters in the presence of the uninitiated that might be inappropriate for them to hear at that time. A Runa can be held at almost any place so long as no females are on the premises or within hearing distance. The various groups will develop various goals and purposes, thus there is no set rule for how a meeting should be conducted. The only ceremonial features are that an

Honor Stone should be present along with a Cross or the Antioch Banner. Each Brother customarily proceeds directly to the Stone and Banner (or Cross) upon their arrival, and salutes as described in the Third Initiation. Each Brother salutes again as he leaves.

Spring and summer are pretty much devoted to recruiting, instruction, discussion and planning. Autumn and winter are given to Initiations, the active pursuit of goals and objectives planned during the spring and summer.

FOLKSTAG. This is a holiday observed on November third, the feast day of Saint Hubert of Liege, patron saint of hunters and foresters. It is held, of course, on the edge of a woods. A large Oak tree is the center of the event. A Cross or Antioch Banner is hung on the west side of the tree, a long table is set up on the west side. At the center is placed the Raven's Bread surrounded by whatever other foods are brought. It's basically a big picnic devoted to games, competitions, music, poetry, exhibits of craft work, plays and the like. Competitions include archery, sling, quarterstaff, falconry, foot races, spear throwing and…if you're lucky…a real live boar hunt; the first to draw blood is designated the Master of the Hunt that day. The last to draw blood, or who makes a fool of himself, gets the pig's tail.

At mid-day, all the Companions are called to the table. ("companion" means "those who share bread". In this case, all Huntsmen, apprentices and Elders.) The Altmann or Anwalt takes up the Bread and says, "This is the Raven's Bread, the Bread of the Oak, the Bread of Honor, the Bread of the Sicarii, the Bread of the Huntsman. Never to be eaten under a roof or without a blessing. Never to be shared with an unbeliever." He then breaks the bread in half and hands each piece to an Elder saying, "Share this with your companions and families and be blessed."

NOTE: The people are encouraged to dress in the ethnic hunting costumes of their ancestors, whatever that nationality may be. Also: no items bearing the name or logo of any commercial manufacturer or merchant is permitted on the site.

Folkstag also serves as an opportunity for delegates from other Hunts to visit, get acquainted and discuss matters of mutual interest in a relaxed, festive and private context.

TENDING THE FIRE. It is a custom among the Brothers of the Order to go to the woods from time to time to renew their experience with Tending the Fire. This is a personal and casual undertaking. It is conducted in whatever manner and with whatever degree of formality the Brother wishes. It is good to spend a few hours or a few days just Tending the Fire. A great many problems are spontaneously resolved, puzzles seem to find answers, insights are gained, direction is found, purpose is renewed. It serves as a kind of retreat from the world, a time to pray, reflect and gain strength.

A good many instructional exercises have been developed for teaching and training and testing new apprentices. We will get into those in the next section; I choose to reserve this section for those things which I am personally convinced are of ancient origin. One such exercise is what is known as Jury Stones. These are three small stones, one red, one white, one black (or a reasonable facsimile thereof). The idea is to give these to an apprentice with the instructions that he should use them to help make decisions. Rather than analyze a situation, rather than resort to intellect and ego, the apprentice is to learn to commit himself to casting these stones to make the decision for him. The white stone is "yes". The Black stone is "no". The red stone is the "decider stone". The question is asked, the stones are cast like dice, and whichever stone is closer to the red stone determines the course of action. The apprentice will have to commit himself, on his Honor, to follow the dictates of chance in this. This is a great exercise in learning humility and keeping one's word. After he has worked with the stones for a time, his mentor (mentor, teacher, sponsor, counselor…they all mean Anwalt), then explains to him that if he can learn to trust his fate to such a stupid and foolish thing as three little colored stones, he can certainly learn to conduct his life by the principles of Honor and the Word of God! The lesson generally sticks.

TOKENS. Anything and everything which serves as a reminder of the Order, hunting, Christianity, Honor, true Manhood, one's loyalties and beliefs are called "tokens". Brothers are expected to make an effort to surround themselves with these tokens. This may consist of furnishings and decorative items, art, and the like in one's home. Personal adornments such as a cross, ring, rune stave, weapons (when and where they can be carried or displayed), a Tatstock or Stammholm. (Again, illustrations of these last two items are shown in illustrations at the end of the book.) Tradition and experience has shown these to be powerful in their ability to remind and reinforce one's loyalty to the principles of honor and the Order.

SUPERSTITIOUS OBSERVANCES. That's what I call them! Nevertheless, because they are traditional, they are passed along to each new generation and are expected to be observed willingly as a point of Honor. They are as follows:

First, never make the sign of the Raven in a mirror. I don't know why.

Second, never allow yourself to be completely naked at any time. Anything will suffice to prevent this; a cross around your neck, a wedding ring, even a tattoo (a tattoo of an Odal rune on the left chest is popular).

Three, keep your hair cut reasonably short or keep it tied up.

Four, never insult or abuse a Raven, crow, jackdaw, magpie or blue jay. And never kill one UNLESS it is illegal to kill one, then you may kill one. But be sure to leave a bright new coin in his beak and take some of his feathers to display. Otherwise, if you wish feathers to decorate with, rely on road kill.

And a Fifth, you should always name your daggers, especially your Initiation dagger. Names are NOT to be given to other weapons. Only a straight double-edged blade is a dagger. No single-edged blade is a dagger; it isn't even considered a weapon, it is a tool. A dagger is never to be used for camp work; not to be used to cut leather or rope, not to be used for digging or cutting wood, not to be used for preparing food or eating, not to be used to skin or dress an animal taken in hunting. It can be used to dispatch a wounded animal. It can be used to deliver the coup de grace for an enemy. A single-edged blade used as a weapon is a disgrace and an insult. The single edge turned to an enemy also turns a blunt edge to you. Only a coward uses such as a weapon. Curved blades are considered evil, especially if it is a single-edged curved blade. (I suspect this comes from fighting the Saracens during the Third Crusade. Moslems used curved daggers and curved, single-edged swords.) Owning swords is also frowned upon. Swords are thought to give rise to ambitions unbecoming to a Huntsman. The short hunting sword is permissible, but not the long sword. The dagger, in medieval thought, was the archetypal symbol of true Manhood and mercy, hence it was often called a "misericorde" (the relief of suffering). The sword, on the other hand, was seen as an instrument of justice instead of mercy, and also the symbol of oppression.

This ends the traditions of strict observance. The next section is comprised of more flexible teachings; wisdom, insights, personal perspectives, the results of my own research, analysis of the psychological and or spiritual meanings of our teachings. I will attempt to present the essence of what I have learned over the past thirty some odd years. It is open to opinion and debate. It includes both what I was told and what I personally think.

Wisdom of the Hunt

THE LIFE OF HONOR

Before I begin, let me point out a natural fact; learning seldom takes place in one lump. Most things in life are learned a piece at a time. We pick up a fact, store it away in our memory someplace, later on we pick up another bit of information. We learn by what we experience and what we hear. It all sort of collects like autumn leaves along a fence line. Then, at some point, it all comes together in a moment of sudden insight; the pieces fall together and we have one of those rare moments of "enlightenment". That's really the best way to learn something, by your own intuition, inductive reasoning if you will. And that's the way I will present this material; a piece here, and another bit later on. Just thought you'd like to know that there really is a method to my madness.

Let's begin by asking the question: What is a man? I mean a MAN, a "real Man", a True Man? Is it being old enough to vote? Is it being big and tough? Is it being old enough to make all your own decisions, having a job and a home of your own? Is it being smarter than others? Is it the ability to "make babies"? No, there's always someone bigger than you, with more money, brains, talent, education, influence or determination. And even a dog can be a father!

And how does one become a "man"? Join the Green Berets, get married, become an Eagle Scout, sign with a major football team? None of the above, I'm sorry to say, only the Life of Honor can do it for you. Just because you call yourself a Man, just because the law defines you as a man, just because others think of you as a man, none of that will do the job. Every male has to be trained, tested and certified by a jury of his peers. Does that make a college fraternity or a street gang qualified to make a man of you? No!

Every male is BORN with a sense of Honor, a sense of what's fair and equitable. They may never learn its value or how to exercise it in their own life, but that's what it takes. And again, a qualified jury of one's peers must certify that you are indeed a fully initiated, qualified man.

Let's look at the issue from a totally pragmatic point of view; a True Man is self-reliant, trained, tested and initiated into a social context (a culture) of Honor…no matter what he does for a living. He is committed to principles by which he lives. These principles help him to survive with honor. These are qualities that allow him to provide for himself and others without appropriating or endangering the means of survival of those around him. A True man can and will go so far as to relinquish his own life and property in order to protect and assure the survival of others. But it goes further than that; the initiation process is an almost mystical, magical experience.

A truth spoken may have a certain impact on a person, but a truth experienced gives the full measure of its reality. To read about war gives us no real understanding of war, only battlefield experience can do that.

Let me interject a note to my fellow Huntsmen who may still harbor doubts about setting our traditions down on paper for the world to read. What I have here is very much like the label on a bottle of vitamins; just reading about what's in the bottle won't help the reader, even if he's a pharmacist or physician, one must still actually TAKE the medicine in order to feel the benefits of it. Those who ridicule vitamins will never take them, those who need the vitamins will be the only ones who bother to open the bottle. Thus, there is no danger of weakening the power or effect of the Initiations or teachings.

And for those critics who think I'm describing a "cult" or religion, let me point out that the Order is no different than any other professional group of Christian Men. We are, in that one respect, much like any other club, fraternity, association or group of Christian Men. We are Men who associate ourselves together in order to apply Christian principles within the context of our particular profession, skill, or calling. In this regard we are no different than an association of Christian athletes…although I think you'll find that the benefits derived from our Brotherhood are vastly superior to any such group or club.

Man is a part of Nature. He was neither created nor fitted to flourish in cities. Cities are the invention of those in rebellion against God and Nature, an attempt to close ourselves away from God and the natural order of the Universe. We have rediscovered the Primordial Sanctity of Wilderness. Wilderness is conducive to the spiritual life. Cities corrupt our relationship with God, nature, each other and our own inner selves. Man was granted dominion over nature. This is both a gift and an obligation. Man has abused, dishonored and abandoned that responsibility. Domesticated man is subject to constant and needless discontent in life, what Thoreau so aptly called "lives of quiet desperation". Domesticated man is utterly blind to the advantages, the serenity, the strength, wisdom, contentment, beauty, truth and majesty of nature. Oh yes, we may visit a National Park and be awed by what we see, but we are not "connected" to the place or its true presence, we see and feel it as an outsider only. It's not unlike a hungry beggar staring through the window of a bakery, he can see it and smell it, but it doesn't fill the emptiness in his gut.

The Hunt (and remember, I'm not really talking about hunting necessarily), is a way of experiencing life as a part of life. Initiation is a catalyst to change. It doesn't force a change, it doesn't cause a change, it only allows change. Some changes are immediate, some gradual, some felt by the initiate, some only after others have become aware of the change that has taken place in him. Change will occur naturally, comfortable. These changes make you what you ought to be, and that turns out to be what and who you really always wanted to be, but didn't know it. It's often described as a sense of having "arrived"…finally! You discover that you have everything in life you want and all that other "stuff" was truly superfluous and no longer matters at all.

We don't read much about the Royal Huntsman in literature or history, but the Huntsman was an official member of every king's court. The Huntsman stood in the shadows and watched the king, he noted his character and demeanor. In fact, the Huntsman's evaluation of the king was the final authority. The Huntsman was a professional; an unparalleled expert in reading tracks and understanding clues to the nature of his quarry. This ability sharpened his perceptive abilities in gauging the character of men as well. The Huntsman was the first to detect flaws in a ruler's character. He could see when something was amiss, mischief was afoot. He read the signs in a man's eyes, tone of voice or a turn of phrase. To a great extent, the Huntsman was the king's alter-ego.

The Huntsmen, as the master of his art, presided over the Royal Hunt. It was he who orchestrated a hunt. It was he who instructed the king and his courtiers in the rules and protocol of the hunt. The Medieval Hunt was a highly formalized, even ritualized, event. But anything could happen. Into this rigidly ceremonial sport was injected the unpredictable element of a wild animal fighting for its life. It was in exactly this context and environment that a man's true nature would reveal itself. The heat of the chase, the confusion and distraction of the contest brought out and displayed one's true character. The Huntsman would detect every wrong move, every infraction of the rules, every lack of courtesy, anger, impulsive behavior, cruelty, conceit, egotism, rudeness, loss of self-control and inability to act decisively in an emergency.

In the context of a Royal Court, the king could easily control circumstances, could act out his intrigues and plans circumspectly and with contrived diplomacy. In the spontaneous and dangerous context of a hunt, his weaknesses and flaws would show. In all this the Huntsman is the Watcher. It is he who weighs the King's character and skill. The traits revealed in the hunt will manifest in the king's role as leader of his people. All the members of the hunt looked to the Huntsman for an accurate assessment of the king's character and traits. If the Huntsman seems disappointed or embarrassed by the king's performance, then the King bears watching. If the Huntsman is perceived to have withdrawn his respect and favor from the king as a hunter, the courtiers will almost certainly turn against the King as a leader. As the king judges the people, so the Huntsman judges the king. And the Judgment of the Hunt is final. Is it any wonder that so many ancient kings had fatal "accidents" while on hunting trips?

The king knew full well that he was being evaluated. The king couldn't refuse to go hunting, that would only stir up suspicion. Nor could he rid himself of his Huntsman in order to employ one more favorable to him. Nor could he employ a huntsman of such low ability as to not detect the king's poor performance. Again, the Huntsman was very much the king's alter-ego. Neither could he hope to bribe a huntsman; such an undertaking would almost certainly be discovered, and no self respecting huntsman, conscious of his Honor and high calling, would consent to bribery. The king must be a good hunter or the king must die. 'Tis more noble to depose a tyrant than to be a king.

I once saw an interview with a former professional purse-snatcher. Once, while stalking a potential victim, someone else beat him to the target. Angered, he pursued the interloper, retrieved the lady's purse and then RETURNED it to her. He said it was the first good thing he'd ever done in his life. His self-esteem shot through the roof. He gave up crime and became one of Curtis Sliwa's "Guardian Angel" crime fighters. I thought at the time, he knows just a little of what it's like to be a Huntsman. But the real point is that he didn't need anyone to pat him on the back to raise his self-esteem, he didn't need anyone to pump up his ego by telling him he was a "worthwhile" person, he needed to do something in order to have self-esteem, to find himself, to have a purpose in life.

Women nest, men quest. Men hunt, women gather.

Good manners with little education will always take you further than lots of education and no manners. It isn't brains that counts, it's character. A man with good manners seems refined. A man with no manners seems more stupid than he may actually be. And certainly his education seems wasted on the wrong person.

The Hunter/gatherer life seems precarious to domesticated people, but the fact is that in all but the very worst droughts hunters fare better than their agrarian neighbors. In Botswana, on the fringe of the Kalahari desert, a quarter million cattle died in one of the worst dry seasons ever to strike South Africa. Farming tribes were starving. Then the Bushmen, who plant no crops and raise no cattle, came to the rescue. The women of the Bushman tribe showed the farming wives where to find wild plants and nuts while the men provided wild game meat. In the Real World, the Hunter/gatherer is the more stable economy.

Truly, the first shall be last and the last shall be first. As the Raven left the Ark before the Dove, so the Raven shall come after the Dove at the end. Jeremiah 16:16

When I speak of the "Real World", I will always mean Nature. Forests, fields, deserts, mountains and valleys are the Real World. God created man to live in a garden, not a house. Try not to be too dependent on civilization.

In the Real World opposites often meet, they often share certain characteristics. The same is true in Holy Scripture. The Hebrews were forbidden to touch a leper for fear they would contract the disease and die. By the same token they were forbidden to touch the Ark of the

Covenant lest they die. The utterly profane and the utterly Holy are both lethal. Much as God loves us, we are told that to look upon the face of God was to die. Saint Paul speaks of his weakness being the source of his strength (II Cor. 12:10), you will find many such para-doxical statements in Scripture. Here is the Mystery and the Power.

The Hunt teaches us to look for parallels, similarities (rather than differences). Expect inexplicable correspondence; what's known in Medieval literature as the science of signatures. This is what Carl Jung meant be synchronicity; everything is connected to everything else, we can gain insights about one thing by watching something else. The cor-respondences don't always have to be logical...in fact, they often aren't. It is enough that they exist at all.

Who can claim the special protection and favor of the Hunt? All female children of a Brother, all male children of a Brother under the age of fourteen. Wives of Brothers, all kinswomen of a Brother not under the protection of a husband or other adult male. Who can be granted the special protection and favor of the Hunt? Any male under fourteen or over the age of fifty who requests it. Any female (not under the protection of an adult male) who requests it. The Brother to whom the request is made must confer with the others of the Hunt and the matter must be agreed upon, then that person is given a Rune Stave to wear bearing the Raven's Track Rune (usually known at "elhaz"). Every Brother should be eager to render aid to anyone in need, but only those who bear the Raven Track come under the special care of the entire Order.

Never fear crossing the threshold of Initiation, internalizing the Real World makes the mundane world better too. It becomes more alive, more colorful, it takes on greater meaning. The mundane world will actually change for you, not just in some vague personal, subjective way, but in actual, measurable ways. Remember, the mundane world as it exists, is only the product of our collective consensus. Every fact of our society began as an idea in one person's mind. Reality is agreed upon and expressed accordingly. By tapping into the Real World we become conduits from an archetypal realm of Honor, romance, idealism and chivalry. The mundane world is nothing like we think it is, it is a sham! Most of us are living out someone else's dream. Someone else said we should live in square boxes, wear these styles, pursue these goals, behave in this manner, and we have simply complied like good little consumers. When I hear businessmen talking, I hear conversations that hearken back to the conspiracies of the Hanseatic League. When I hear of war in Bosnia, I hear of the continuing struggle between turncoat Christians who accepted Islamic conversion by the sword and those Christians who remained loyal to Christ; a war that has not ceased in 600 years. When I go to the Wildwood, I experience the Real World which hasn't changed in millennia.

There are some who, by whatever coincidence, have experienced the Real World spontaneously, usually for a mere moment, the twinkling of an eye. They know not how to hold it, to return to it, to prolong it, or what to do with it if they could. This is the role of Initiation.

What the alchemists called "earth, air, fire and water" we know as "Blood, fire, storm and stone." These are the elements of the Real World.

A society or civilization is not so much language, frontiers and economy. If they are to survive, thrive and renew themselves, they must first be a culture with coherent and fixed spiritual frontiers.

Cedar fire, Oak and Stone, straw death, blood runes, ancient vows, the four griefs and the fifth grief. Blood, fire storm and stone. Here the past and present meet to become the endless future. Odal, heritage, what we receive from our fathers binding us to our ancestors, completing the cycle. In the Initiation we meet our ancestors, we become our ancestors. We do not find meaning by being other than our ancestors but in repeating the cycle, perpetuating the Tradition, proving our worth to carry it forward as they have passed it on to us.

For a man to say is his heart, "I will be a man of honor" is totally inadequate, because the operative word is not "honor", it's "man". Our society speaks too easily of "Great Men". There have been few Great Men in history. Most were the pawns of fate, many were secretly guided by others, or motivated by greed and egotism. Only those men were great who were True Men. Nature and circumstance produce very few of these. Only a valid Tradition of initiation can accomplish this. And just reading about Initiation isn't much help; it can't be analyzed, it must be synthesized, then internalized.

Words of wisdom: Deny everything you are accused of and you will end up being suspected of everything. Readily confess occasionally and you will be readily believed when you deny culpability.

A Warrior with honor can't survive long in an unprincipled world. Only a Huntsman has the imagination, the wisdom and flexibility for it. He is a Trickster. The Trickster has his dignity and Honor, but he is creative and cunning in coping with the mundane world, and he can do it without violating the principles of honor. Jesus told us to be wise as serpents but innocent as doves.

Wisdom is the ability to gain insight into a problem and the will to apply that insight to its best advantage, whether mending harness or a personal relationship, whether raising kids or voting in an election. Wisdom is the ability to appreciate life and to be grateful for it, and to inspire that wonder and gratitude in others. Wisdom is good humor. Wisdom is the power to convince with a bark instead of a bite. Wisdom is the power to be at home in the Real World while present in the mundane world. Wisdom is silence when you know the answer, because the questioner doesn't really want the Truth, or isn't ready for it. Wisdom is knowing that the ability to do a thing doesn't necessitate doing it. Wisdom is knowing that not all mysteries and secrets should be revealed. Wisdom is a sense of perspective, balance, principle, trust, loyalty, compassion, dignity (self-respect without being proud). Wisdom is knowing the difference between humility and humiliation. Wisdom is giving advice without attachment to whether or not the advice is taken. Lastly, Wisdom is not always intelligence, only the practice of virtue. Such practice will lead a man to sound decisions. Such a man may not be witty or knowledgeable in a formal sense, but he will be respected and honored. Best of all, he will be a Good Man.

The U.S. Forestry Service has adopted the Valknut as its official symbol! How ironic. Was it a deliberate decision on someone's part or was it chosen on some deep subconscious level by archetypal energies?

Pope John Paul II is living proof of the debt the Catholic Church owes to Conversion by the Sword. Had the Teutonic Knights not Converted Poland, and most of the pagan tribes in the Baltic region by force, there might very well be no Pope John Paul II.

Without doubt, some readers will say the Brotherhood has a doctrine in search of a "proof text". I understand that concept and have heard many "hobby horse" doctrines and interpretations of Scripture that fit that definition. Such doctrines and teachings often have a certain appeal and seem to make a lot of sense, but upon closer examination of the Scriptures, I have found they are utterly insupportable; whole denominations are founded on unfounded doctrines!

In this instance, the evidence and proof are there. These are not "secret" doctrines, nor obscure or irrelevant teachings, they are IGNORED prophecies and doctrines. Jeremiah 16:16, conversion by the sword and the primordial sanctity of wilderness are presented in a clear and straightforward manner and confirmed by other Scriptural

Witnesses. The problem is: These prophecies and Scriptures aren't popular!

I'd like to point out that in Jeremiah 16:16, God doesn't say He will replace Fishermen with Hunters, He only says that AFTERWARD (after He has called many fishermen), He will call many Hunters. The evidence suggests that Hunters will never replace Fishermen, nor will Hunters become Greater than Fishermen, only that Hunters will be called last. Hunters will always be a tiny minority; "gleaners" if you will, who come along picking up stragglers and compelling them to attend the Great Feast. It might be well to remember that it took a long time for Jewish Christians to accept the idea that gentiles could be Christians, it's no surprise that Fishermen have a hard time accepting Hunters. But what then shall we do with the clear Scriptural evidence?

Our mission is simple: (1) Initiate males into the life of Honor and True Manhood. (2) Strengthen the sick and wounded. (3) Convert pagans. (4) Protect and defend Christendom. And (5) Fight against the forces of antichrist at the appointed time.

Now what's wrong with that? Who could possibly take issue with those goals? The only point that might be challenged is the first; that we might be saying, "No Christian is a True Christian or a True Man unless he has been Initiated into our Order." We're not saying that at all. The facts, however, are these: There are plenty of 16 year olds who are True Christians, but there are plenty of 30 year hold True Christians who have no more maturity than 16 year olds. Can a True Christian grow into True Manhood without our help? Certainly. Can they benefit from the help of others? Certainly. Can our Order provide that help? Absolutely, and in a methodical and deliberate manner, with profound results.

A Brother of the Hunt is a Man of Honor, he has already experienced the Little Death; he is a walking dead man. It's the "Doc Holliday effect", you can't win against a man who has nothing to lose.

With nothing to lose, there is nothing but joy, death has been faced down and is in the past. All loose ends are tied up, all business appointments are canceled, all that matters is one's Honor and Loyalty to God.

What good is it to teach children to pray when they aren't taught to say "please" and "thank you"? They may call God "Father", but they don't bother to call their own father, "Sir".

Most prayers, reduced to their essentials, say, "Please don't let 2 and 2 make 4."

Psychological research has shown that the subconscious mind really doesn't seem to know the difference between a symbolic event and a real event. Researchers have found that actors playing a role tend to experience all the same physical and emotional symptoms of the characters they portray, even their blood chemistry coincides with the physical and emotional state of a person who is actually undergoing the events depicted. The same is true in Initiation; symbolic acts have exactly the effect they portray. The effects of Initiation are almost certainly even more profound for two reasons; first because the Initiate has a desire for the effect to take place, and secondly that the events portrayed are of a carefully formulated and orchestrated ARCHE-TYPAL nature.

The Primordial Sanctity of Wilderness is a far-reaching subject. I will only try to give you a basic understanding of the concept.

Adam and Eve may have been created to live in a Garden, but the next generation was born in the woods! Wilderness is our natural home. Recall that it was Cain, the murderer, who took up farming and built the first city, and was the "father" of all the arts and crafts of technology. Look at the many positive examples we have: Abraham was called out of the city of Ur to live in the Wilderness. Moses met God in the Wilderness. The Hebrew Children wandered forty years in the

Wilderness to be purged and purified. Virtually all of the Patriarchs and Prophets lived in the wilderness. John the Baptist lived his entire life in the Wilderness. Jesus went up into the Wilderness for forty days immediately following His baptism in preparation for His ministry. Jesus frequently returned to the Wilderness to rest and pray. Saint Paul retired to the Wilderness of Arabia for about three years before beginning his ministry. The twelfth chapter of the Book of Revelation speaks of a mystical "woman" who flees to the Wilderness and is protected there. Isaiah (40:3) calls Believers to the Wilderness. John the Baptist repeats that call in the Gospel of Matthew (3:3).

It is important to understand that in both the Old and New Testament, there are separate and distinct words that are translated "the world". In the New Testament, for instance, the most common word for "world" is KOSMOS; this refers to the world of human beings, the way we have arranged things, our human society and life style. Almost without exception, the term KOSMOS is used in a negative sense. When Scripture refers to Nature or the Earth, the word is GE, from which we get such words as "geology" or "geography". It isn't the physical world that has a corrupting influence, Nature is still the best place we can be. It is "city" life that tends to corrupt and distance us from God. As I said earlier, this is a vast subject for study.

Who was John the Baptist? Scripture tells us he was "in the wilderness" from his birth until he began his ministry. How can this be? Where did he live? Who took care of him? Most scholars believe that he was either an Essene monk or a nazarite. As these same scholars admit, there are some very serious problems with both of these ideas, both from the Scriptural and historical standpoint. There is, however, one circumstance that fits perfectly. John the Baptist was raised in the Rechabite tradition!

John didn't drink wine or eat bread; neither did the Rechabites. John wore clothes made of camel hair, the Rechabites were herdsmen who raised sheep, camels and horses and lived in tents made of camel hair cloth. They probably also wore rough camel hair coats. As expert horsemen, the broad leather belt bound the midsection to protect the stomach and kidneys of a rider. John preached in the Wilderness. Why? The greatest audience of sinners lived in the cities, there was plenty of water in the cities for baptisms, so why not go there? Rechabites despised cities and avoided them as much as possible. Read the 35th chapter of Jeremiah. You will see that while the Rechabites took the Law of Moses further than the Law demanded, yet God approved of their chosen life style, and blessed them. God promised that the Rechabites would continue forever and indeed they have; there are still bands of Rechabites living today in the deserts of Mesopotamia and Yemen.

But John was the son of Zacharia, a priest in the Temple at Jerusalem; surely he was a Levite! Not necessarily or entirely. Jewish tradition tells us that Levites married daughters of the Rechabites (apparently they were distantly related), thus Temple priests could be descended both from the tribe of Levi AND the Rechabim. The Christian historian, Hegesippus, tells us that "One of the priests of the sons of Rechab, the son of Rechabim, who are mentioned by the Prophet Jeremiah" cried out in protest against the slaying of James the Just. Thus it is probable that John was related by blood to the Rechabites. Because John was dedicated to God at birth, his parents may very well have put him in the care of Rechabite family members to raise him in the Wilderness in the strict religious traditions of the Rechabites.

Historical accounts tell us that the Jews in John's time saw the Rechabites as extremely holy, and that they symbolized the pure worship of God by living in the Wilderness. It is said that the Rechabites struck a note of nostalgia and spiritual guilt in the hearts of the city-bred Jews.

Jesus was John's cousin, which may or may not mean that He Himself had Rechabites among His ancestors. In either case, Jesus certainly appears to have endorsed some of their teachings in His own personal conduct.

What have the Rechabites and their traditions to do with our Order? Only this, that they are a positive spiritual example for us, that John was almost certainly a living endorsement of their teachings and life style, and that Jesus, Saint Paul and the other Apostles may very well have had strong sympathies to their Traditions. It is interesting to note that Saint Paul was a tent maker by trade, so were the Rechabites. It may very well be that Saint Paul had a long and close familiarity with the Recharbites in that he may have purchased camel's hair cloth from them to make the tents he sold for a living.

It should be enough to point out that all of archaeology, anthropology, psychology and biology agree…human beings are HUNTERS by nature! Just the fact that our eyes are set in the front of our heads, as with all other predators, and that our eyes must work in concert looking at only one thing, is powerful biological evidence. Creatures that don't hunt have their eyes on the side of the head to watch in different directions, always alert for predators.

For millennia our ancestors lived as hunter-gatherers. In the next stage of our development farming became dominant. Many peoples built their societies around settled agrarian life. This period is often said to have been ruled by a matriarchy. The feminists dote on that idea; they paint it as a time of peace and plenty. In fact, we now know that there was virtually no such thing as inter-tribal conflict (war) until tribes had something worth stealing…a surplus of food! In any event, it is certain that whether women ruled or not, when marauding animals or thieving tribesmen threatened the crops, it was the men with their experience of hunting that took up their spears and bows to protect the fields. And when the crops failed or were stolen or destroyed, these same hunters went back to the woods to get meat for the winter. Eventually hunters became a specialized labor force hired specifically to protect the fields and herds while others concentrated on planting and harvesting. In time these erstwhile hunters, turned security guards, lost their sense of community; becoming too distanced from the life of the

Hunt, they also lost their sense of honor. These former hunters were no more than hirelings with weapons. They discovered that the mere presence of these weapons and a belligerent and intimidating attitude could result in higher wages. In time, the hired guards began to see themselves as the masters of the village by right of arms. They built fortifications and imposed taxes. The polis (city) was born. From this one word we have concepts such as "metropolis", "police" and "politics". Of course the farmers still needed to protect the crops so they tolerated these arrogant politicians. But no matter how uppity the politicians became, the entire society still knew, somewhere deep down inside, that the politician's power must always rest on his ability to be a good "hunter". The farmers and those in the political pecking order always watched to see that the "top dog" maintained that quality. Hence, those who had retained and maintained the true hunting tradition were always turned to as the experts in assessing and certifying the king's worthiness to rule.

You may have noticed that effigies of knights on their tombs are often depicted with a dog lying at their feet. This was to suggest that they were a good hunter and thus a good leader. Prince Albert, Queen Victoria's consort, is depicted in this way. It is interesting to note that after Prince Albert's untimely death, the only person that could console the queen was Albert's Huntsman...a situation that gave rise to much misgivings among the nobility of Great Britain.

In the twentieth century hunting was greatly neglected by heads of state. Nevertheless, a great many of them made it a point to be seen and photographed with dogs. There is in this the archetypal implication that they are still "good hunters".

Most historians now agree that Teddy Roosevelt was the ideal American president; the one man that was right for the times he lived in. No matter how they justify their opinions, these historians invariably end up discussing his reputation as a great outdoorsman and hunter!

Sports have come to be the standard of success and respect among most men of Western Civilization. But what sport is there that isn't based on the chase and/or targetry? The very qualities of a good hunter! Football is nothing more than a formalized "greased pig" scramble. Perhaps this is the REAL reason a football is referred to as "the pig-skin".

Folk wisdom tells us that "you can't fool kids and dogs". Children are natural born psychologists, they sense when someone is a phony. Dogs seem to have similar traits. We tend to have reservations about people who don't like dogs; even moreso when dogs don't like them!

Robert Bly, author of "Iron John", did rather well in defining the problem of loss of True Manhood in modern society. I've often loaned copies of his book to those whom I wished to introduce to the Order, it serves well enough as a stepping stone. I corresponded with Robert Bly for a time and gave him a copy of another manuscript I had written about the Order. He apparently saw the value of our Tradition and asked to be initiated into the Order. As it happened, his busy schedule would never allow him to visit our area. Our circumstances did not permit us to visit on his home ground, and we were never able to find anyone of another chapter who was close enough or available to perform the initiations for him.

This circumstance brought us to the stark reality of the difficulty inherent in trying to preserve our Tradition. It was painfully obvious that those at a distance (either in time or space) could never be initiated. Over the last seven or eight years, we have brooded much about the problem. At long last an acceptable and agreeable solution has been arrived at. We call it an **Origination Ceremony**. This is what we have authorized:

Any two adult males, over the age of twenty-one, can originate a new chapter if they are unable to make personal contact with an Elder of our Order. First, they must create an Honor Stone (as found in the appendix of illustrations at the back of this book). Then, having studied this book and firmly committed themselves to live the Life of Honor, they may Originate a new Hunting Order. This type of "freeborn" chapter will be known as **"Oskorei"**. It's pronounced OHS'-kor-aye. This is a medieval name applied to a troop of Huntsmen meaning "to step out" or "stride along". In modern English vernacular, it is readily translated as "high steppers". As you may learn, Huntsmen in ancient times, were seen as high-spirited, fun-loving rowdies and show-offs. This would be especially true of young men who had just received their third initiation and been recognized as full fledged professional Huntsmen of an Order.

Once the stone is prepared, they must enlist the aid of an outsider, preferably a man over fifty years old, to serve as a witness. This is the one and only time an outsider is ever to be present at a formal ceremony of the Order. It serves to witness to the world at large that a new chapter has been created and to place a burden of guilt and shame on anyone who originates a new chapter of the Order and fails to live up to the standards set before them.

Following the autumnal equinox and after the first frost, they must proceed to a wooded site beyond any hint of civilization. At midday, or at sunrise or sunset, the older of the two Originators must draw the circle and half-circle depicting the Penumbra. Both should assist in building a small fire in the center of the circle. The Honor Stone is placed in the middle of the Penumbra and the two Originators then sit down cross-legged on each side of the stone, the older Originator sitting facing west, the younger facing east. Each Originator must have a well-sharpened dagger. The older of the two Originators takes the lead; he is to lift his dagger and hold it at eyelevel with the blade flat and horizontal, the edges turned toward himself and his companion. The younger then does the same. The older then says, "BEFORE GOD AND THESE WITNESSES, I PLEDGE MY WORD IN BLOOD TO LIVE AND DIE BY THE PRINCIPLES OF HONOR EMBODIED IN THE CODE OF THE DEATH BOND INSOFAR AS THEY REFLECT THE TEACHINGS OF HOLY SCRIPTURE, SO HELP

ME GOD." The older then takes his dagger and stabs himself in the left chest, scoops up the blood with the blade of his dagger and touching it to the stone says, "AMEN." The younger companion follows along repeating the pledge and the wounding. Laying aside their daggers, they each wipe their wounds with their right hand and clasp their bloodied hands across the Honor Stone saying, "IN THIS WE ARE BROTHERS." This ends the Origination ceremony. The outsider is free to leave or walk away at a distance while the Originators bandage their wounds, put out the fire, scatter the Penumbra and gather up their equipment.

Every Huntsman must initiate or sponsor at least one other recruit. Once another recruit is found and apprenticed, they must each take their turns serving as Anwalt to complete the first three Initiations of the Order among themselves. They are then a fully certified Order and each is a fully certified Huntsman. If at all possible, a search should be made to contact an already established Traditional Order which has been developed by right of primogeniture (the old-fashioned way). Then, by whatever means is available and agreeable, the Oskorei can be interviewed so that it can be ascertained that they have indeed met the criteria in originating a new chapter.

Remember this, and never violate the rule: The Anwalt must always bear the full expense of recruiting, training and initiating new members in the order. Beware of anyone who so much as hints at compensation for his services. It is customary to display generosity in giving gifts to one's mentor, it is equally customary for one's mentor to give gifts to his apprentices. All gift giving is to be a token of friendship and goodwill, never to enrich someone.

The formulation of an Origination Ceremony is a new thing. We have done this and take full responsibility for it. Our reasoning is that an Origination Ceremony is simply striking the fire anew. A new flame will burn as bright as one kindled by the sparks of an older fire. So long as the fire is tended with sincerity, it will burn bright. It is not the Initiator that accomplishes the task of Initiation, he is merely the means by which the Tradition is passed on. It is the dedication and determination of the Questor and intrinsic archetypal power of the Initiation itself that accomplishes the task. There is a great deal to be said for the strength of the right of primogeniture and influence of mystical contagion, but if the hearts of the Oskorei are right, those qualities will become established in them as they are in us. If, however, contact can be made between a freeborn Oskorei chapter and any Elder from a Traditional chapter of our Order...at any time in the future...then the Elder Brother may, and should, present the Oskorei with some token (such as a rune stave bearing the blood of an Elder of the Brotherhood). This will serve to establish and confirm the Oskorei through the principle of mystical contagion.

SACKMAN. This, apparently, is a corruption of an old German word meaning "an expert in some matter". Sending for the "Sackman" was an expression used to threaten unruly children. We can well imagine why.

SICARII. The Brothers have always been fond of heaping names to themselves. I suspect this one was acquired in the Holy Land during the Crusades. When they learned of the Jewish zealots who were known as "Sicarii" because they carried concealed daggers to assassinate Romans during the time of Christ. The parallel to themselves was probably irresistible.

VALKNUT. This is an old German/Scandinavian term. It actually consists of two words; VAL, meaning the dead, and KNUT, a knot or bond. It is pronounced FAL'-kuh-noot.

KINSTONE. Or Kenstone. "Kin" suggests a family member or someone you are related to. "Ken" is a German word meaning "knowledge" or "to know". The Kinstone seems to be an external objectification of one's self.

WOLF TREE. Such a tree is characterized by being twisted. Wolf Trees are never cut. The grain of their wood is twisted and too hard to work with; it has no value for domestic use.

PENUMBRA. This a place where light overtakes darkness creating a half-shadow during an eclipse of the sun. This was a "dangerous" place or condition; things could happen here, things could change at that time or place. Anything that constituted an "edge" was a mystical place; where woods give way to a clearing, the place where the sea meets the shore, the edge of a well, a cliff, dawn, midday, sunset, midnight, a horizon, the cutting edge of a dagger, that place between sleeping and awakening, etc. All of these, and any others you might observe, were considered "The Way Between Worlds".

SUNDOG. A symbol depicting an eclipse of the sun (see illustrations). The moment the sun begins to reappear from behind the moon, also known as a ring star. This is one of those penumbra moments. As a symbol, an inscription written within the band of the Sundog was thought to have great power, thus such an inscription is highly significant. NOTHING is to be placed within the circle of the Sundog symbol…EVER!

The word "sundog" is also applied to an atmospheric condition in which the sun's rays shine through falling hexagonal ice crystals with all of their axes in a position perpendicular to the horizon (a most peculiar circumstance which the ancients surely had no way of understanding, but would certainly have found "significant" and relevant to their concept of being conducive to magical events). When the ice crystal axes are distributed at random, a circle appears around the sun, but no sundog.

The inherent symbolism is interestingly suggestive of a sign of order, harmony and coherence in nature. Thus, the sundog is a symbol of the order of nature and natural balance.

TATSTOCK. This is a tool peculiar to medieval European Huntsmen. The Tatstock is a straight club an inch or so thick and about two feet long. The Tatstock is cut from a tree limb in such a way that a fork about six inches long is left at one end. This "hook" is sharpened so that it serves as a tool. The Tatstock (which simply means "work stick") can be used to turn a carcass over while skinning or dressing it (a skinned deer can be extremely cumbersome and slippery). It is also used to retrieve objects from water or from a tree branch, and can be used to hook and carry something. When not in use, it is thrust through the back of the Huntsman's belt.

STAMMHOLM. Pronounced SHTAHM'-holm. This is an interesting old German word. It seems to mean both a walking staff and a "family tree" or genealogy. It is a badge of authority for any Huntsman and especially for an Elder of the Hunt.

ALTMANN. Pronounced AHLT'-mahn. It simply means "Old man"; the oldest and/or most experienced Huntsman of a Chapter. The Altmann generally presides over ceremonial events and is expected to be a wise but passive counselor.

ANWALT. Pronounced AHN'-vault. The name means "Counselor" or "Advocate". The word is still used in the German language to refer to a defense attorney, one who stands up for someone else. The Anwalt is usually expected to train new recruits, and is a Counselor for the Hunt in a more active sense. He might be seen as "first among equals", as a natural leader of a group of Huntsmen. His office is respected but he has no real authority or "right" to command others. ALL Huntsmen are free and sovereign entities by nature.

HANSE. Pronounced HAHN'suh. It is also spelled "hansa". It means "company". The Hanse is by nature, an evil concept. The Hanse is one of our avowed enemies. More will be said about them later.

An important point which I failed to mention earlier (but that's alright, everything happens as it should, and this serves to draw your attention back to the Third Initiation), is the mask worn by the Altmann during the Third Initiation. This is made of cloth, dark green or gray, cut in a long triangular shape (see the illustration at the end of the book). It only has one opening for the eye, the left eye. The right eye is covered. On the center of the brow is an Odal rune.

Masks are fascinating things; they don't actually hide one's identity, they REVEAL one's identity! In this case, the Altman becomes the archetypal huntsman, Trickster figure, culture bearer, Raven, etc.

As you will learn, if you bother to research the subject, since ancient times and in many cultures, the one-eyed man was significant. He symbolized a man under a vow, one who knew "Dangerous Things", a man with a mission or purpose. Alexander the Great's father, Phillip of Macedon, was known as a one-eyed man. Barbarossa's father was called a one-eyed man. You can find many such examples throughout history and mythology. It is said that King Richard the Lionheart wore a patch over his right eye during the siege of Jerusalem and had vowed to wear it until he had taken the city. He felt he could not gaze fully upon the Holy City so long as it was in the hands of the Saracens.

I have only recently learned that there are other Hunting Orders besides the Orden der Valknut. I suppose I should have guessed as much, but, quite frankly, the idea had never entered my mind. I have now learned that there are other Hunting Orders and they are not all Christian! What their goals or purposes may be I do not know, but if they are not Christian, they should be avoided like the plague.

THE PRINICIPLE OF MYSTICAL CONTAGION is easily explained; given the choice between owning a perfect replica of George Washington's sword, or owning the original sword with all its nicks, scratches, rust and wear, which would you rather have? The brand new replica might be better in the sense of better steel, all shiny and new, but the Original sword is the one that bears the touch of the Father of our Country, it must utterly radiate the essence of who it belonged to, where it has been, the great events at which it was present. To own such a token, aside from any monetary value, would be wonderful, inspiring, exciting and of the greatest significance. This same example serves to explain the perfection of imperfection; all those nicks and dents give it character, you would WANT it to show signs of age and use, it would be perfect...BECAUSE of those IMPERFECTIONS.

In the same way, it is our scars and wrinkles that suggest experience, war stories to tell, character! A lady friend of mine once pointed out that with age, women develop wrinkles, men develop character. She said it, and I won't argue with it.

Interesting point: (one of those "correspondences" or "signatures" or synchronicity events). Every Huntsman has the right to add the letters LH after his name as a title (meaning Loyal Huntsman). In the Runic alphabet, such letters are often combined to create what's known as a "bind rune". The bind rune for LH looks like the Greek letters CHI-RHO, which is a commonly used abbreviation for "Christ", and a common symbol for Christianity.

Another relevant point regarding the symbol of the Sundog is that it perfectly describes the Hunting Order (especially in the modern world). While the sun's face is hidden behind the moon, it is not visible, the world grows dark and cold. However, this doesn't mean that the sun's strength and light are in any sense diminished, merely eclipsed. That one bright point of light which explodes from the moon's rim is proof that the light will return. In like manner, the Hunting orders are eclipsed but not diminished.

And let me add one more point; it is quite obvious that the "star" at the Sundog's rim is similar to a "swastika". I could go into a lengthy discussion on the origin of the swastika or gammadion as it is also know, but I will point out only this: Our Order has nothing whatsoever to do with nazism. The swastika, gammadion or sunwheel, as we prefer to call it, was around long before Hitler. And, as every scholar knows, the black, left-handed swastika (as the nazis depicted it) has always been the symbol of chaos and destruction; a symbol of fear and aggression, the very symbol of death. This swastika was once used to mark tombs and burial urns. The right-handed sunwheel, as we use it, was always the symbol of light, life, good fortune and the natural order of the universe. A little research will confirm this. This symbolism is derived from the idea that the sun was a great ball of fire which rolled across the sky from east to west. If we imagine the flames trailing out behind it as it rolled across the heavens, the flames would spiral away to the left suggesting a right-hand or clockwise turning. Hitler admitted that he deliberately chose the black, left-handed swastika to, as he put it, "Strike fear into the hearts of our enemies." So let us put that subject to rest once and for all; it makes no more sense to abandon the right-handed sunwheel as a symbol of the Hunt than it does to abandon the Cross of Christ just because Satanists use the Cross upside-down as a symbol of their evil endeavors.

I may as well point out that the sunwheel was one of the earliest symbols of Christianity, even before the sign of the fish was used.

The Ancients believed in the elemental nature of Creation. They believed in certain Elemental Powers. I will teach you four such elemental powers and a fifth. I consider these superstitions, do with them as you see fit, however...they do work. (How can I dismiss them as superstitions and yet affirm that they have power? Because I'm a Huntsman, a Trickster!)

There are **Four Powers and a Fifth** such as any Huntsman would find indispensable in his chosen craft. Blood, Fire, Storm, and Stone...and a fifth; the Reconciler of Opposites. BLOOD: This is a blood charm to stop bleeding from even the most severe wounds. One need only repeat this verse from the Bible in the presence of the wound, it is Ezekiel 16:6. STOP! Do not look this verse up in the Bible for yourself. Go immediately to a woman, let her read the above instructions, look up the verse and teach it to you, otherwise it will NOT work for you and you will never be able to teach it to another. I have used this on both myself and others. It does work.

FIRE: This may sound like a curse, but is more on the order of a "banishment". It is as follows, "Thou art tophet! Thou art darkness and a place of burning!" Let's say someone has an unjust grievance against you or someone else, let's say someone has seen or learned something which is truly none of his business and which he might use to cause someone trouble. You might say something like this, "In this matter, thou art tophet! Thou art darkness and a place of burning! Whatever you may know or remember will be wrong. Memory will deceive you and your certainty will fail. Selah" He will immediately begin to re-examine his thoughts and memory to confirm their accuracy only to realize that the more he thinks about it, the more unsure he is; facts begin to contradict themselves, memory begins to stray and fade, uncertainty creeps in and his confidence will consume away. Moreover, others will simply doubt his veracity and reliability. But remember, I said the matter in question must be UNJUST. You can't go around working evil with this or it will backfire on you big time!

STORM: This elemental power serves as fair warning to one who seeks to attack you unjustly, this can apply to a human or an animal, perhaps even to dangerous situations; a violent storm, a raging river, a precipice or other natural danger. It is as follows, "I am (say your name). Beware, farawisi!" The last word is pronounced, FA'rah-vee-see. It is an ancient Viking/Germanic word which simply means, "I know dangerous things". Again, be sure you are not deliberately provoking a bad situation, that you have not knowingly put yourself in a dangerous circumstance or behaved foolishly. This is not a license to be stupid. In fact, it may not turn the dangerous animal, person or situation aside, it may only serve to give you the "edge" to win. At the very least, it will put YOU on notice that you are about to learn a valuable lesson!

STONE: Sometimes when you take a deer in the hunt, you may find a white stone in the deer's stomach. This is known as a Madstone. It is very valuable. When anyone is bitten by an animal suspected of being rabid, the stone can be placed on the bite to test it. If the Madstone clings to the flesh, the animal was indeed rabid. The Madstone will continue to cling to the flesh for a time and then fall off. The Mad-stone must then be placed in a bowl of milk whereupon the milk will begin to turn green. After a few moments the stone should be removed, washed in clean, cold water and placed in a second bowl of milk. When the milk ceases to turn green, place the stone again upon the animal bite. Repeat this procedure for as many times as the stone clings to the victim's flesh. When it no longer clings to the flesh of its own accord, the poison is gone. There are those who say the Madstone will work on snake bites and infected cuts as well. I do not know, I was not taught that.

THE RECONCILER OF OPPOSITES: The fifth element, which makes all the others work, is the principle of attraction; that which binds the Universe together. The opposite force would not be repulsion but chaos, the power of evil. That which binds may be understood as LOVE. The following oracle, if taken seriously enough to put it to the test, resolves questions and issues for which there seems to be no common ground or satisfactory answer. Many European folk cultures know this method. It is as follows: Take a Bible, hold it in your hands and pose the matter in question, allow the Bible to fall open at random while your eyes are closed. Place your hands on the open pages and, by feel alone, choose a place to point your finger. Then open your eyes and take note of the word, sentence or verse you have chosen. If you are sincere and truly seek enlightenment on the matter, you will have your answer. If you are behaving frivolously and experimenting, you may find that your finger points to a long list of "begats", a blank space on the page, or a passage consisting of a sharp warning.

RECRUITMENT. Do not attempt to bring just anyone and every-one into the Brotherhood. Not everyone is called to the life of the Hunt. There are a number of reasons for this, suffice to say, this is so. Let your intuition guide you. You will find those who are not suited are strongly repulsed by the mere hint of the subject, do NOT press the issue. If you find one who is genuinely interested, at some point ask him about the wound to his right leg. You will often find that he has, at some time in his life, usually before the age of fourteen, had a memorable injury to his right leg. This is a sure sign of a natural-born Trickster personality who will make an excellent Huntsman. However, even then, you may find that he has a powerful aversion to becoming a Brother of the Hunt. Many such men, by the very nature of being a Trickster, are opposed to "joining" things. They may also have some secret, which they instinctively know disqualifies them; some sin which, intuitively they know they would have to confess, give up and/or relinquish their "bragging rights" about. Others may actually have such a collection of mistakes and such a personal history of intrigues and bad involvements that even the first initiation would throw their entire life into confusion in the process of unraveling all the stupidity and nonsense of a lifetime. These people are simply unwilling to be put through such a radical straightening-out process.

On the other hand, they may be willing to endure the ordeal, but it will take some time, and the initiation process may have to be strung out over a period of years in order to allow the process of repair, correction and healing to take place.

I forgot to mention one further detail regarding the fifth initiation, which I do not recommend, (wasn't that convenient!) The Initiate must also inflict a dagger wound to his left chest, and the cut is not to be dressed until the initiation is completed or terminated.

When you were a child, did you learn the value of "king's-X" to win immunity in children's games? Many of us did, certainly the older generations knew it well. It is an identifying code that has leaked into general use. In ancient times the women and children of a Huntsman's family could cross themselves and cry out, "King's Cross" or "king's X" to warn a potential attacker who they were. To insult, abuse or attack a person under the protection of the Hunt was to incur the wrath of every Huntsman who learned of it. As Huntsmen served a Royal house, a Noble family or an Order of Warrior Monks, it was suicide to give offense to a Huntsman's friends or family.

Among Huntsmen themselves, to cross the fingers and lay them over one's heart was a signal that danger was near, that he wished to speak in private about some matter, or to simply identify himself to someone he thought might be a fellow Huntsman. The proper response to this signal is to ask, "What ails thee, Brother." (Ah, shades of poor Parsifal, who never learned good manners!)

Another custom that has leaked into general use, is the wink of an eye to a companion to put him on alert that a joke is about to be played, something is afoot, beware, pay attention, follow my lead, or just to identify oneself as a fellow Huntsman. It is a sign of the Trickster, the One-eyed Man.

Would you believe that the very concept of the comic book superhero is based entirely on the Huntsman? The mask, the super powers, the enemy of the forces of evil; they're all founded on the universal and archetypal personality of the Hunter. The Lone Ranger wore a mask to identify himself more than to hide his identity. Many super heroes had side-kicks who provided comic relief; these are the archetypal fools, the shadow of the Trickster figure. Some super heroes had no side-kick, these generally wore black to denote the companion shadow. Super heroes are usually nomadic, having no fixed abode, or they live in some secret place; a cave, a mountain top, a forest. And they seem to have no visible means of employment…not unlike the way society views Hunters! We ARE super heroes, we do have phenomenal powers, we are dedicated to stamping out evil, we do move unseen in daily life. I'm frankly surprised that no one has gone straight to the source and invented a comic book hero based directly on the Huntsman, especially the Dread Huntsman, who is the professional assassin, the angel of death, the original "ninja" warrior.

Another aspect of modern literature and entertainment is the "conspiracy theory". This is not the work of fictional imagination or paranoia. I can assure you…because I personally KNOW…there are very real and active evil conspiracies at work in the world. Virtually every conspiratorial group you have ever heard of is based on actual fact. Even within national governments, there are so-called "rogue elements" which use their position and power to manipulate and direct world events for the benefit of a few leaders who dream of world domination and their own self-interest. Many of these groups work in concert with each other, some work against each other, some are entirely unknown to others. The only one I can name without signing my own death warrant is the Hanse. The World Trade Organization and many other such groups of Merchant Princes, Robber Barons and Lords of Commerce, are the modern descendants of the Hanse. The very nature of the Hanse is conspiratorial. A corporation orchestrates the power and resources of many and directs it as the will of a single entity. The only goal of the Hanse is to make and control wealth. Business seldom exhibits a conscience; corporations exist for the sole purpose of making money, and they will do what they must to make it happen. Evil as the Hanse is…and they are desperately depraved…others make them look like angels of mercy.

If indeed we are Lords of the animals, then how shall we claim those rights and responsibilities? By the act of Largesse. Upon the day of the Autumnal equinox, at the very hour of the equinox if possible, one should betake himself to the woods, to a lake or pond. There he should scatter food, such as oatmeal or bread crumbs on the water, then place some on a low hanging tree limb, then upon the ground and, making a hole in the ground, place some of the bread or meal therein and cover it up. Last of all, he himself should eat some of the same bread or oatmeal. In this he has shared his own food with the fish, birds of the air, beasts of the field and those creeping creatures, which live in the earth. If none but ants consume his gift, it passes to all other creatures through the natural food-chain as the ants become food for other creatures who, in turn are eaten by still others. In eating the Huntsman's food, they place themselves in his debt and in his service. At the same time, the Huntsman is put in remembrance of his responsibility to use the resources of nature, which God has put at man's disposal in a wise and reverent manner.

As a free and sovereign Elder of the Hunt, I have the right to create a new custom, which I have done. It was not presented under the heading of strict observances because it is not yet in universal practice. It is however accepted within our own local Chapter of the Hunt. It is this: In the second, third and fourth initiations, the Initiate is presented with certain gifts in the course of the formality or following the formalities of the initiation. You will observe that no such gift is made following the first initiation.

Some years ago I took up the practice of the Prayer Rope. This is an Eastern Christian practice not to be confused with the Roman Catholic Rosary. The Prayer Rope which I use is slightly different than that used by the Eastern Church. The Prayer Rope is made of black wool yarn consisting of thirty three knots, one for each full year of Christ's life on Earth. A wooden bead is placed between the twenty ninth and thirtieth knots to mark the beginning of Christ's ministry. The Rope terminates in a knotted cross which completes the circle. The Cross stands at the beginning and end of the Rope. The Prayer Rope is held in the left hand and the knots are counted off by the fingers as the so-called Jesus Prayer is recited mentally: "Lord Jesus Christ, Son of God, have mercy on me a sinner." Thirty three repetitions of the Jesus Prayer completes the circuit. The Prayer may be said as often as you like at any time or place. In fact, the Jesus Prayer is less a prayer than a confession of faith; every word of the prayer is a statement of one's belief. It says Who Jesus Christ is, who we are, our spiritual condition, His ability to save us and our dependence upon his Grace. It is NOT a repetitious prayer which many Protestant Churches denounce. True, Jesus spoke against empty repetitious prayers...such as the heathen pray, but we are also told to pray without ceasing, to pray repeatedly, and we have the example of Jesus Himself, who prayed THREE times in succession "that this cup" (His crucifixion) might pass from Him. There are a number of benefits arising from the use of the Prayer Rope which I will not bother to enumerate here. I have also experienced some rather amazing results in the use of the Prayer Rope. I find it very useful and have chosen to present it to each Initiate upon completion of the First Initiation. An illustration of the Prayer Rope appears at the end of the book along with information regarding where these unique Prayer Ropes can be found.

Any dagger, as previously described, will serve the Huntsman. However, there is an archetypal Huntsman's Dagger, it is called an **Ox-tongue**. The design is simplicity itself. The Ox-tongue is a broad blade; two to as much as three inches wide and about seven to nine inches long. It is made with a full fang and the handle consists of hardwood scales (sometimes rosewood) and is fitted with many brass rivets. It has no hilt (in the sense of a cross guard). The haft or handle curves inward on each side so that the midpoint of the handle is only about an inch and a quarter wide. The pommel or butt is the same width as the blade. I have found, in the course of my own studies, that this copies one of the most ancient and widely distributed designs, going all the way back to the early bronze age. The broad blade suggests the shape of the penumbra, the way between worlds, as indeed it is for those who are the recipient of its work. A Viking ship was also shaped like a penumbra; while it may have been a precarious way to travel, it gave a man a place to stand between the sea and sky and by entering therein, the adventurer might pass from one end of the Earth to another…literally from one world to another. The Hanged man also enters the penumbra when he hangs between the Earth and Sky and the world is turned upside down.

Try not to be confused, bored or disgusted; I'm not trying to teach you a bunch of facts and figures, rules and regulations. I'm trying to help you make a little breakthrough. I'm trying to teach you a world-view, a mindset, a perspective you may never have even considered before. It's really worth the effort.

MALE AGGRESSION: This is actually an amazingly simple subject with a good many facets. I'll try to present it in small pieces. When there are no girls around to impress, when the intended victim has done nothing worthy of being attacked or intimidated, the bully is acting out his latent homosexual desires. Oh yeah! Macho guys won't like hearing that! But the fact is, our ancestors had a lot more insight into unconscious motivations than we might imagine.

Most gay guys that have come to terms with their homosexuality display very little in the way of aggressive behavior. Unfortunately, there are a very great many guys who have completely repressed their homosexual inclinations and it acts out in aggressive behavior. Aggressive behavior is a means of compensating for feelings of insecurity, fear of being seen as the weakling they really are, a fear of letting their gay tendencies slip out. Just consider the kind of abusive language they use on their victims: "F*ck you, ya little faggot!" "Hey, you want a piece of me!?" I don't think I really need to run down the long list of commonly used abusive expressions, you get the idea, they are all veiled expressions of homosexual focus and desire. A bully is really wanting to commit homosexual rape. In fact, the bar brawls he gets into are exactly that! Guys who beat up on girls are acting out their resentment in being dissatisfied with heterosexual relations. Child abusers are a bit more complex, but they begin with the same latent homosexual urges plus a desperate sense of inadequacy, low self-esteem, inferiority, gross juvenile-level immaturity and a number of other components.

Guys like to pretend that acting out is somehow "manly". In fact, acting out only proves they aren't man enough to master their male hormones. It's not a surplus of testosterone, it's a severe retardation of masculine development.

Homosexual behavior is rampant in our prison system. We just automatically assume that's because these guys don't have access to women. Did it ever occur to you that not having access to females is just a very convenient excuse for this collection of very aggressive guys to openly engage in homosexual behavior? Think about it!

This brings me to a related subject; the CURE FOR CRIME: Why do people commit violent crimes...or even white collar crime, for that matter? It has far less to do with need or greed than we think. It's primarily about EXCITEMENT! These guys are bored, they have no "drama" in their lives. They feel (and ARE) inferior, insecure and weak. They want to be the center of attention, they want to be noticed and admired. They want others to fear them. About five percent of those in prison are mentally deranged. A somewhat larger percentage are sociopaths (that's also a form of insanity which is generally not considered "insanity"; sociopaths know right from wrong, they just DON'T CARE!). The vast majority of prison populations are just desperately immature. They are WEAKLINGS! Among women who commit crimes, about ninety five percent commit those crimes in concert with, at the behest of, or due to the indirect influence of a male. The other five percent are insane.

So, while male hormones aren't the real cause of criminal behavior, it can be the means of curtailing crime. No, I'm NOT going to recommend an initiation procedure or a specialized psychiatric treatment. The Old Brothers had an instant cure for rogue males: CASTRATION! It works, it has always worked, and it will still work. Look at the history of castration; The very word, "eunuch" (a castrated male) was synonymous with "steward" in ancient times. It was known that a eunuch was docile, submissive, honest, and clear-thinking. Yes, castration seems to clear the hormonal "fog" from their brains. The Greeks held eunuchs in high regard as military officers; they tended to be clear thinking strategists, didn't panic in an emergency and were very reliable. Castration does for human males what it does for animals. Castration turns a raging bull into a docile steer. A wild stallion becomes a well-behaved gelding. It's the earliest known form of brain surgery.

There's a further aspect; those known to be eunuchs are avoided by aggressive males. Former friends and fellow criminals simply don't want to be seen hanging around with a "gelding"…it might be "catching", besides these slow-witted criminal types think of a eunuch as a kind of "queer" and being friendly with one might cause others to think they are "queer". In any event, the eunuch really doesn't care much for crime anymore.

Now in the matter of sociopaths, castration doesn't always work (no one seems to know why). For those who persist in criminal behavior there is yet another remedy: surgical blinding. It is painless and very effective. The blind criminal cannot deal dope, shoplift, rob banks or write bad checks. He can be put to work making brooms or some such to provide his own support.

You may well be aghast at these suggestions, but it's really only because you aren't familiar with them or their effectiveness. It's my understanding that eunuchs enjoy the kind of peace of mind and tranquility that a normal male can't even imagine. Eunuchs can be gainfully employed and lead a perfectly happy life; it's instant rehabilitation. So which is better, a prison full of violent people just waiting for parole so they can commit further crimes, or a docile, productive citizen? Which is more cost effective, a one-hour surgical procedure or twenty years of housing, feeding and guarding violent males? You think the death penalty doesn't scare criminals? I guarantee you the possibility of being castrated…even by a painless medical procedure…strikes terror into their black little hearts. Just ask a criminal type which he would prefer, life in prison or the death penalty as opposed to castration.

If you meet a bear while out hiking and you have the urge to scream and run, just make sure you scream and run TOWARD the bear. You can't outrun a bear. Your best chance of surviving the encounter is to scare the bear away. It may not work, but it is far more likely to work than running away from the bear. The same principle works with aggressive males. Never run away, never back down, never stand your ground either. Don't look for trouble, but if you can't avoid it, go to it! When confronted by a "bully", the last thing he expects is for you to advance toward him. It's very disconcerting to have someone move toward him while speaking in a conciliatory manner. He may not run, but maybe you'll get close enough to sucker-punch him.

And when you hear a noise in the house at night, don't hide under the covers, you'll only become increasingly frightened, get up and go to the noise, you'll be amazed at how your apprehension instantly begins to fade.

WHAT IS ELECTRICITY? Are you aware that nobody really knows what it is? We know how to "call it up" (that's called "generating it" by means of esoteric rituals based on the alchemical philosophy of physics). We pretty much know how it will behave once the demon of electricity has been conjured up…except it doesn't ALWAYS behave as it should. Properly controlled, it can do an astounding array of work for us; it can make ice cubes, heat water, carry messages through the air, cause the internal combustion engine to work, do intricate mathematical computations and many, many other things. In fact, our whole civilization is the product of electricity (named perhaps after the mythical Greek character, Electra, who helped her brother murder their mother?). But the simple fact is, those who don't know how to control the demon of electricity may easily be killed by it. Am I being silly in calling it a demon? Consider this; the power of electricity promises much, but for all the myriad inventions it empowers for good, the vast majority of them are also used for evil. Virtually every electrically powered invention can and often is used for illegal, immoral purposes. Perhaps this is the real goal of the demon of electricity. Maybe it's time we re-evaluated ALL our modern technology!

No matter how difficult the task, the decision to do "the right thing" is always harder than actually DOING "the right thing". Once we are committed to doing the right thing, the act of doing right is often surprisingly easy...even joyful...and certainly the more productive.

Remember my little essay at the beginning of the book, "Who'll Tell the Kids?" There's a further message there, it follows right along with the Biblical teaching in Deuteronomy 32:6-7, which urges us to "remember the days of old...ask your father...". It shows us in no uncertain terms that the ancient wisdom is often the best. There's a reason these ancient truths have been around so long...they work!

It took me a long time to figure out why I find Yuppie types so disgusting. They seem so clean and wholesome, so in-step with everything. And then one day, it finally hit me...they are utterly untested, untried, unproven. Virtually everything they do, believe, and think is mere theory. There opinions are based on academic studies and opinion polls. They are adamantly for this or that without having any real understanding or experience of the matter. Yuppies are just a collection of upper middle class fads. They are a fabrication of secular self-righteousness, pop-psychology, politically-correct attitudes, and fuzzy-minded liberalism. Lots of trendy tastes and interests with no real-life experience or comprehension of what it's all about. And they are so hypocritically tolerant of everything...except an opposing opinion.

Speaking of animal rights activists (HA!), their basic premise seems to be the "Value of All Life". What exactly constitutes this value they speak of? They are concerned about people who wear leather shoes and fur-coats, they look down their noses at people who eat meat and especially those who HUNT! So, what is it? Is it domestic animals versus wild animals? Apparently not, they seem to feel just as strongly about dogs and cats! Do cock roaches have rights too? If all life is valuable and to be protected, then rats are equal to cats. In fact, if a "soul" is a soul, then even germs have rights! In which case, we need to protect the AIDS virus from being stamped out…even a virus has a right to make a living! Doesn't life, liberty and the pursuit of happiness apply to ALL life forms? Either it does or they need to reconsider their basic philosophy.

An Orthodox Rabbi recently went on record saying, "The Revelation of what's truly evil or good comes from God alone." His point being that it is EVIL for activists to equate animal life with human life. The Catholic Church has also stated officially that because animals have no spiritual responsibilities they have no spiritual rights. God made man Lord of the Animals to do with as seems good to us, with this one stipulation: It is evil to harm an animal for the shear pleasure of causing pain. We are not to be cruel to animals, but we may kill them as humanely as possible to protect our own life and property, for food or other resources. The Bible is rather succinct in the matter of Hunting; The Bible says things like, "Don't kill anything you don't plan to cook" (…don't plan to utilize) Proverbs 12:27. The Bible also tells us that the righteous man regardeth the life of the beast. That's rather simple, straightforward and comprehensive. Animals are a resource, not to be wasted or abused. That doesn't protect them from being made into fur coats or hamburger. So get over it, you people! When God says a thing is okay, you don't have any right (animal or otherwise) to say something different!

ODINISTS. I have known for some years that there were people running around loose who called themselves "Odinists". I never took them seriously…who could!? But it has just come to my attention…this past week, to be specific…that these "Odinists" are much greater in numbers than I imagined. They also seem to insist upon their sincerity in worshipping the Norse Gods. The problem is this: They use much the same terminology we do. One might easily conclude that we and they are birds of a feather. Nothing could be further from the truth. While it is evident that our Order is descended from an ancient Hunting tradition and that certain of our customs are derived from customs and usages of the Middle Ages, we are very much CHRISTIAN!

One might just as well conclude that we are pagans because we are descended from pagan Europeans. Just because we are their offspring doesn't mean we are pagans. The fact that we have inherited their light skin coloring, continue to speak their "pagan" Germanic languages, wear long pants (a surefire mark of paganism by ancient Roman standards), and continue to call the days of the week after pagan gods...Tyrsday, Wodensday, Thorsday, Freyrday...doesn't mean we endorse pagan religion. A vast number of our customs, manners, holidays, alphabets, languages, and attitudes are derived from our pagan ancestors. Shall we allow ourselves to be tarred with the same brush just because a visible few try to resurrect a pagan religion? Surely not. And shall we abandon all our social conventions and create new ones just to accommodate these pagans? Absolutely not! Why should we have to change ourselves when it is they who are the evildoers? Granted, sometimes evil, immorality and foolishness are so institutionalized within a culture that radical changes must take place when Christianity is introduced. But, contrary to what 19th century missionaries thought, God is NOT an Englishman, and an entire native culture doesn't have to be abolished to make the world safe for Christianity. Indeed, if Christianity is culture-bound or culture-specific, it is not the True Religion! If Christianity can be so threatened by the common customs and usages of local culture, then Christianity is weak indeed. And, if Christianity is in fact culture-bound, then we should all be learning to speak Aramaic and living in Judea.

I'm probably too old to learn Aramaic or Hebrew anyway, besides, the New Testament was written in the Pagan Greek language, using the pagan Greek alphabet. It gets worse: The pagan Greeks called upon their pagan gods using the word theos, after they converted to Christianity, they began to call upon the True God using the word Theos.

Their moral standards may have changed, but their cultural norms remained pretty much intact.

The traditions of the Hunt have been around a lot longer than ancient Greece and Rome, but is now most decidedly Baptized and Christianized. If this is not so, then what shall we do with American Indians who convert to Christianity and continue to speak their native tongues, tell their ancient folk tales, practice the ancient hunting wisdom they learned, sing their native songs, even sing praises to God in the style of Native American culture? And what shall we do when they put on feathers and celebrate their tribal ceremonies and dances? Oh my! But wait…despite differences in language and custom, do they not believe in the same God that we do? Of course!

Perhaps some will say that we shouldn't quibble over our customs and usages, we should be willing to change or de-emphasize certain aspects of the Order to avoid comparison with some heathen cult. But, I say again, why should we yield an inch of ground to a bunch of silly play-acting pagan wannabes? I will add this: any chapter of the Hunt that wishes to disguise their traditions to avoid ridicule is free to do so, just be careful not to throw the baby out with the bath. Remember, we were a Hunting Order first; men who hunted for a living. We evolved into a guild of professional Huntsmen who, like all ancient guilds and professional fraternities, sought to preserve the traditions of our craft and gain the favor of the gods current at the time. When Christianity came, we continued being Huntsmen practicing the customs and skills of our trade while abandoning paganism in favor of the True Religion of Christ.

Forgive me if I seem to belabor the subject, but that's exactly what I intend to do! Americans respect and admire the Great American Cowboy. But that's certainly no blanket endorsement of everything they were and did. We may imitate their better qualities and even model our own lives and interests after them, but without taking on their less desirable traits. Today we may even wear our cowboy boots to Church without anyone thinking we are uncivilized or pagan! In like manner, we respect and admire our Hunter ancestors and the traditions of the Hunt.

Let me get very specific about any parallels between our Hunting Order and "Odinism". Every Loyal Huntsman converted to Christianity right along with the House he served, or he was no Loyal Huntsman at all! Any pagan group that tries to lay claim to any aspect of our tradition is a blatant liar! It is evident that there are Hunting Orders who are not Christian, these can only be "dogs who have returned to their vomit"! They are agents of evil, serving the various conspiracies that abound; they are apostates who have renounced Christianity to serve their own selfish ends.

Now, having established our right of primogeniture, let me proceed to take away the very basis of the "Odinist" cult. It should be obvious to any rational, intelligent person who knows beans about mythology that Odin was no "god" at all! Even in the time Snorri Sturluson wrote the Heimskringla, it was understood that Odin was never a "god", but a folk hero who had been blown out of all proportion. Indeed, Odin was probably never a real person at all, just a fictional figure constructed from elements of the Hunting Life. The very name "Odin" is derived from the same source as the present German word for "woodlands" or a forest. Odin, Votan, Wodan, Woden, they're all derived from "Walt", meaning a forest, or "Waldung", meaning woodlands". Wodan…Waldung…not a lot of difference, is there? The Aesir were the gods of nature and the wild world, just as the Vanir were the pagan gods of domestic life; the plowed field, crops, cattle, good health and the like. Odin was a patch-work personification of admired qualities: The intelligence of Ravens who led hunters to game, the ferocity of wolves, the authority of the strong man with a spear, the gravity of death which made men reflective, the dedication of the one-eyed man who never wavered in his course of action and the wisdom of the hanged man (but to make him a "god", he was depicted as hanging on the tree nine days, three times longer than a human was expected to). And let's not forget that Odin was also the patron 'god' of MER-

CHANTS, which brings us to the ultimate meaning of the entire Viking movement; which was not conquest and glory but the means of opening new trade markets or outright thievery…whichever proved to be the more convenient at the moment…and which evolved into the Hanseatic League, the grandfather of today's World Trade Organization.

The traits, which were grafted onto the figure of Odin, were the traits of Nature in the Wild; traits to be understood, not necessarily emulated. Mastered, not obliterated. Held in balance, not perverted. Worked with, not twisted. Controlled but not enslaved.

The True Huntsman was the True civilizer, not some sort of "wild man". He was the True culture-bearer. It was the Huntsman's duty to civilize men. Perhaps you think this is somehow a contradiction; in like manner, it is the hunter that has always been the True conservationist…not those agrarians who pollute the land and destroy it. And so it was in ancient times. Who do you think taught the warrior to track an enemy, to lay an ambush, to survive in the wilderness? It was the Huntsman.

Consider the legends of the Berserker warrior. The Berserker had the supposed "gift" from Odin to become a Berserker in battle. The Berserker was a formidable enemy; impervious to fear or pain. He stripped off all his clothes and rushed wildly into battle slaying everyone within reach. Some Berserkers wore a wolf skin or bearskin (hence the name "Berserk", meaning bear shirt) to bring on the Berserk rage. Historians tell us that it was the very presence of Berserkers in society that perpetuated and gave some degree of credence to the cult of Odin and the Norse gods. They also point out that the presence of Berserkers was also a very intimidating factor which tended to make others shy away from investigating the new Religion of Christ. Had the Berserkers never existed, the Norse religion would have died out centuries earlier. As you might imagine, Berserkers were not at all popular; in fact the Norse religion was never all that influential, except among a few fanatics and anti-Christians. Nobody ever "loved" the Norse gods, they were feeble, unreliable. Norse mythology depicted them as capricious and desperately flawed; prone to lying, word-breaking and other all-too-human traits. Odin was the only god who had anything at all to offer men, and even that came with too high a price. The warrior who became a Berserker understood that at some point Odin would exact a price for his "gift". That price was the "war-fetter". As surely as the "battle-frenzy" made him invulnerable, the "war-fetter" would paralyze him and guarantee that he would be slain by his enemies. These Berserkers, with their seemingly supernatural battle-frenzy, were nothing more than institutionalized thugs whom nobody liked, except warlords who used them as "terror tactics". And what's more…the very trait that brought them so much fame and power was nothing more than the results of FAILED INITIATION! Yes, the battle-frenzy is what is known today as "bush fever". No matter how civilized a man may be, anger him or frighten him and he will bare his teeth. This only proves how thin is the veil of refinement and domestication. We are all, at heart, creatures of the forest. We are predators. And, one who becomes lost in the woods will often shed his domestication and revert to his animal instincts. This is a natural survival trait. Unfortunately, those not trained in the ways of the Wilderness don't simply revert to the wild, they "go wild". They will actually run and hide from potential rescuers, and will fight like a wildcat against those who attempt to catch them.

What was once known among Berserkers as the "war-fetter" is commonly and jokingly referred to today as "buck-fever". Many uninitiated hunters will freeze-up when they have a game animal in the sights of their rifle. This is also why so many people freeze when confronted by a wild animal. Again, it is the results of failed Initiation (or a total lack of initiation).

Now you know why Huntsmen are taught never to be entirely naked, they fear going berserk…and it's easier to do than you might imagine. Anyway, the Berserker was never a very good fighter, he was far more frightening than effective.

The prevention or cure for either Bush-fever or Buck-fever is the same; a piece of food held in the mouth. Huntsmen were always advised to carry cheese or honey cakes for that very purpose (never meat). It's thought best to simply hold the food in the mouth or to chew it lightly and avoid swallowing as long as possible in crucial moments. Never go into the woods or into battle hungry.

Huntsmen understand that the forest is a great teacher (even the word for counselor, "Anwalt", which means an advisor or advocate, is made up of two words, "an" meaning "into", and "walt" meaning "the forest"), but while we respect the forest, we're not so stupid as to worship it.

If indeed these Odinists believe in a spiritual world, then they need to shake off this fantasy and wake up to the fact that Norse mythology is exactly that...a romantic folk tale with no spiritual power. While it may have a certain cultural impact, if it is not placed in service to the True God of the Universe, then it is utterly futile. If they are so immersed in their beliefs, then surely they have read enough to realize that many of the more "theological" myths about the Norse gods are late (VERY late) inventions intended to compete with the Truth of Christianity. Baldur, the "saviour" god, was a feeble attempt to create a Christ-like myth. And certainly no one can avoid seeing that the "apples of Idunn" are the "apples of Eden"; the fruit of the Tree of Life which gives immortality. And so many other myths are just veiled poetic references to everyday things; Sleipnir, the eight-legged horse of death, suggests the funeral bier carried by four men, one on each corner; eight legs worth! As to Odin's ultimate worth, normal men, about to go into battle, called on Ull, the god of the Hunt, to protect them from the weapons of their enemies. They knew very well that what they had learned as hunters would probably serve them better on the battlefield than anything Odin could do for them with a "battle-frenzy". Let the Odinist chew on that.

In summation, as I have said before, WE are Christians. We utterly repudiate paganism; it was nothing more than entertainment and comic relief for the dark ages. "All good things are wild and free...give me for my friends and neighbors wild men, not tame ones."—Henry David Thoreau

As discussed above, the Huntsman was concerned about "going wild". He was probably far more concerned that others perceived him as a potential Wild Man. The Huntsman himself was very much in control and at home in the Wild.

The Middle Ages were rife with superstition, not the least of which was the idea of the Wild Man, which pervaded all of Europe. In fact, the Wild Man is a universal archetypal figure common to all cultures in all periods of history. Europeans, however, seem to have been especially fearful of the Wild Man. The forest itself was a foreign place. No civilized man would even think about going into the woods alone. It was understood that only four kinds of people went into the forests alone; hermits, madmen, outlaws and witches...and a fifth: Huntsmen!

"Madmen" included the fabled Wild Man, werewolves, cannibals and all sorts of monsters. Yes, cannibalism was actually rather common in Medieval Europe. Any self-respecting man who valued his reputation and his life was careful to guard himself against any such accusations. While hunting was a very important activity, it was always conducted in groups, never alone. The Huntsman, by virtue of his skill and duties, was often alone in the woods. This "bothered" many people. It was understood that Wild Men had no refinements, therefore the Huntsman had to be a shade more refined than his town-dwelling peers. Wild Men had no names, thus our habit of accepting, even heaping to ourselves, whatever names and titles we can. While it was often the style to wear long hair, cutting and dressing hair was a bit of a nuisance, the Huntsman was always careful to either keep his hair cut or to bind it up. Wild, tangled, unkempt hair said two things: This man is uncivilized and/or he has no one to care for his hair for him (as would be the case with a Wild Man, madman, witch, outlaw, hermit and so on). The Huntsman's situation was all the more precarious in that while these others were social outcasts who preferred to remain hidden in the forest, the Huntsman lived in both worlds, and the forest was truly understood to be ANOTHER world. In fact, the forest WAS the Other World of Celtic lore, where all manner of strange and perhaps supernatural creatures dwelled. Thus, the Huntsman lived on the EDGE; always between two worlds, at home in both. He must be the most companionable of all men to avoid suspicion.

Civilized man, if he is to ever understand his most profound inner significance and purpose, must be in touch with Wilderness. Modern man complains of the discomfort and inconvenience of the outdoor life, this is because he is so utterly out of touch with Nature and his own true nature. There is a great subconscious agony in all men who are not united with Nature. The True Huntsman hears Nature, he feels the Wilderness, he comprehends the speech of silence and can answer all the questions posed by Civilization. The Huntsman is the very key and keystone of civilization. The culture that loses touch with the Wild is doomed to sink into decadence.

In ancient times, storms were thought to be the "Wild Hunt". That was an easy assumption, after all, the Ravens were seen flying before the storm as it approached and seemed to be leading it, just as they led Hunters to game. This brings us to the Legend of the Storm Raven. Birds commonly ride the strong forward air currents at the leading edge of an approaching storm. Large black Ravens often dominated the flock and observers concluded that the Raven caused the storm. Legend says the beating of the Raven's wings stirred up the storm which he was then trying perhaps to escape. The lesson was that it is wiser to BE than to DO. It seemed obvious that all the Raven had to do to escape the storm was to come to rest somewhere and the storm would cease. The application of this lesson in human affairs is this:

The only thing any human being wants is contentment. The problem is that we over-complicate contentment. For the most part, contentment is simple creature comforts...nothing more! The difficulties arise not so much in attaining comfort, but in seeking to insure CONTINUED comfort. Humans can contemplate the possibility of future eventualities; we can imagine misfortune and death. This creates insecurity; fears of what might go wrong, fantasies of what we might do to prevent the loss of comfort, schemes to insure on-going comfort and contentment. We begin to contrive ways to enhance, augment, expand, improve or re-new comfort and contentment. In short...we seek control, we become ambitious! Immediately we begin to lose sight of present comforts and become fixated on future comforts. We invent "deferred gratification" wherein we sacrifice the comforts we have for some hoped for future contentment. In seeking this ever-expanding control, we not only ruin our own contentment but everyone else's.

Jesus taught us to, "Take no thought for tomorrow, sufficient to the day is the evil thereof." But we really don't believe that, and we certainly don't practice it. Ambition is an ugly thing, it always seeks to raise us above our peers. Don't get me wrong, we should all strive for excellence in whatever we do, but the desire to be better than others (as opposed to being better than WE presently are) is wrong. Most guys have already dodged the bullet as soon as they read the statement. "Oh well, that's all I'm trying to do!" In fact, most of us are tainted with greed, envy and ambition...we just like to call it "trying to get ahead."

Learn to be still, let the quarry come to you. Be still and perhaps the storm will cease, or at least pass on by. Be still and contemplate what you already have; learn to be ACTIVELY grateful, count your blessings, marvel at how you've gotten so far in life without having been eaten by something. Gratitude is the real means to contentment. As Scripture says, "Be still and know that I AM GOD."

Here's a question you may have wanted to ask (I know I did!). If the Teutonic Knights had become so corrupt, why didn't their Huntsmen, the Orden der Valknut, simply denounce them and withdraw from their service? See, isn't that a good question!? Just the sort of question a modern guy with no sense of Honor would ask! It was because the Order had made a commitment; they were bound by honor to carry out their sworn duty to serve the Knights and the Crusading vocation.

Well, couldn't they just NOT initiate new Huntsmen into the Order? That would prevent other men being caught up in the same dilemma and the Order could have ceased serving these corrupt Knights by simple attrition. An equally good follow up question! Typical of people who look for loopholes! But remember, initiating new Huntsmen and passing on the Tradition was also part of their duty both to the Knights and to the Order itself. All they could do was to carry out their sworn duty, try to be a positive influence on the Teutonic Knights, and wait for them to reform or disintegrate.

It's important to recall that the Huntsman's duty to endorse or denounce their master according to his conduct in the Hunt never presented itself in this situation. The Teutonic Knights were monks! Normally monks weren't even allowed to eat meat, but the Pope had granted the Military Orders an exemption to that rule. However, monks were also forbidden to hunt! And since the Knights didn't go hunting, they were never on the Huntsman's "turf", and couldn't be legally "evaluated". (I've often thought that the real reason Churchmen weren't allowed to Hunt was this very factor; to prevent their being too closely scrutinized by Huntsmen.) Thus the Huntsmen carried on the Hunt as a purely utilitarian matter of providing meat for the Knights' table. Even when the Knights began to decline and fell on hard economic times, they refused to discharge their Huntsmen. Clerks, servants, even cooks and grooms were discharged from service, but the Knights kept their Huntsmen, partly for the sake of obtaining meat, but almost certainly for the sake of their image as well.

It has come to my attention that most people are now of the opinion that courtesy is part of some kind of "belief system", and that we have no right to impose our "beliefs" on other people. When did civility become part of an arbitrary belief system? It's not a religion or a political opinion. Civility is the price of admission to CIVILIZED SOCIETY! It is not optional! Civility is like personal hygiene; it's good for your health in and of itself, and it keeps us from being a stench in the nostrils of our peers. Bad manners, like bad hygiene, has natural consequences, you can become unhealthy...even dead! It can keep you from getting that job, promotion, date, invitation, help, respect, concern or other opportunity that you hoped for...and may otherwise be qualified for. Strangely enough, the same trendy, politically correct people who become very vocal and confrontational about racism, sexual harassment and smoking, happily tolerate or engage in profanity, discourtesy and abuse of their peers' personal dignity. Why? This behavior is all of the same cloth. Think of the ill will, revenge killings and wars that began with a personal lack of courtesy toward someone. Nobody lives in a vacuum. How you behave effects everyone. To betray the rules of social decorum is a form of treason. Yes, I said TREASON! It undermines and poisons our society as much as drugs, crime or foreign subversion. If you're concerned about self-esteem issues among children, why aren't you the least bit concerned about the rules of common courtesy? Anyone who violates the rules of courtesy is either desperately ignorant or INTENDS to damage the fabric of society. That person must be called to account instantly; the same as if you caught them painting graffiti on a Church, setting a fire or stealing.

We all agree that we have certain civil rights...doesn't the right to civility count? Don't we have a right to our personal dignity, the right to not be "dumped on" with a load of offensive language or information or attitudes? I know from experience that very often a teenager's antisocial behavior stems directly from the fact that they don't know how to exercise good manners. They become frustrated at being unable to define, find or establish their own place in society because they don't know the proper behavior for some given circumstance. They have an abysmal ignorance of the rules of courtesy and hospitality. They don't know how to conduct themselves in polite society, especially in relation to adults, authority figures and superiors. They are anxiety ridden and choose to bluff it out or act out. They would rather deliberately disregard social convention than to be exposed as having no social skills.

There's an old saying that is an absolute truism: Good manners with no education will take you further in life than education with no manners. It's obvious; people with good social skills are perceived as being more intelligent and educated than they really are. Those with no manners are perceived to be far more ignorant and uneducated than they may actually be.

Good manners works in both directions. The courteous person is exalted right along with the person who is the recipient of courteous behavior. I have won more arguments with courtesy than I ever did with wit! I have gotten further in life with courtesy than my limited education alone could ever have taken me. Get a clue, people!

The social engineers pontificate from their ivory towers, and the Government propagandists constantly flog us with the same brainwashing message: All our social problems, all our economic problems, all our political problems…even your spiritual problems…can be solved with just a little more money and a little more education. Except, we seem to be getting in deeper by the day. Am I lying? You know it's true! So why hasn't more money and education solved any of these problems? Because that was never the solution! The solution was always CHARACTER! Unfortunately, you can't buy character and you can't learn it out of a textbook. Character comes with training, just like good football players, artists, musicians and pilots. It can be part and parcel of any educational curriculum…IF the powers-that-be want it! And now we get closer to the root of the issue; the powers-that-be DON'T want it! They want a society in chaos. You can't declare martial law unless there is rioting in the streets, you can't institute a police state unless you can stir up enough crime to justify police state tactics.

You can't get the people to follow you unless they are frightened enough to accept a fool for a leader.

Character is as easy to instill as reading and writing…oh, I'm sorry, I forgot, the-powers-that-be don't want you to read or write too well either, it leads to creative, analytical thought and they certainly don't want the public doing any of that! Wake up, people! They're turning you into a mindless mass of consumers, "useful idiots" (as Lenin so aptly put it). America doesn't need more welfare and government funded programs, it needs to stand on its own hind legs, develop some character, get a sense of HONOR, be responsible for its own well-being, take responsibility for its actions (both individually and collectively), bite the bullet and "quit yourselves like men", as the Apostle Paul urged.

The way to contentment is to be content. Start right now, right here, with what you already have. If you can find no satisfaction in what you have, are, and do right now, then don't expect to be happy with what you are shooting for in the future. Contentment isn't about "stuff", it's about YOU!

The cynic is defined as a man who knows the price of everything and the value of nothing. He ridicules and mistrusts everything. He is motivated by fear and insecurity. The Trickster must never be mistaken for a cynic. The cynic gloats when he's proved right, the Trickster is deeply disappointed.

Yes, the Trickster, like the cynic, often probes, challenges, examines and investigates. But, unlike the cynic who only wishes to make others as small as himself, the Trickster looks for strengths and hopes to stir up that strength; to challenge character to assert itself or, at the very least, to expose hypocrisy; to force his opponent to face his own inconsistencies, contradictory views and lack of courage, and to take a stand. The Trickster doesn't ridicule in order to tear down a person's self-esteem, but to provoke a defense; to reexamine his own position, or to take a position, assert and defend it. The Trickster is a sparring partner; he punches the other guy to make the other guy better, quicker, smarter, stronger, tougher. You can learn more things, and more things of real substance, from a Trickster's questions than you can from a teacher's instructions. People instinctively suspect the Trickster and his motives. He's accused of being an enemy or an adversary, even a "devil". But his is never the case. His tricks, riddles, sly questions and open ridicule is always intended to expose fear, weakness, error, hypocrisy and ignorance…and indecision…especially indecision. Don't be too quick to doubt what I'm saying, later on I'll present you with a very thorough discussion on how Jesus Himself was the Master Trickster figure, and why not…wouldn't the God of Creation be the master of His Creation? An archetype (such as the Trickster figure) is just a formula, a plan, a schematic, a blueprint for accomplishing a task. And where there is a blueprint, there is a Draftsman who knows the blueprint perfectly.

Face it, human beings don't like to be challenged, that's why they don't like the Trickster. The Trickster makes them feel inferior and foolish. That's why the Trickster has so often been cast in the role of a "devil". But remember, Satan does what he does in order to mislead, corrupt and destroy you, while the Trickster is, again, a sparring partner who is trying to TRAIN you. The Trickster is part of every human personality (some more than others). Just take an unpopular stand and insist on your position. You will see the Trickster emerge in those around you; they will tease, probe, ridicule and pester you. But, if you stand firm, in short order, these same adversaries will come over to your side, or they will at least defend your right to your views. And above all, no matter where their sympathies may lie on the subject in question, they will have a much higher respect for you as a Man.

When you were seven years old, could you relate to girls? While some boys that age have a certain "inclination" toward girls, the vast majority of seven year old boys find girls repugnant. Do you recall that attitude? Even if a seven year old knows all about girls and sex, of what real use is it to him, he's not likely to enter into a boy/girl relationship with any likelihood of becoming a father.

When you were fourteen and puberty had struck, your whole outlook and understanding of girls changed. You KNEW what girls were all about; you had a radical change of heart, your eyes were opened, you were "enlightened". Still, could you have seriously contemplated becoming a father and the head of your own household? You might be able to "make babies", but are you really qualified to be a father? Could you have successfully handled the job? Almost certainly not. You could barely comprehend the concept.

When you were twenty-one, and perhaps married, a father and the head of a household, could you relate to what it meant to be an old man, an Elder? Could you really imagine what it would be like to slip into old age and infirmity? Could you imagine being the Patriarch of your Clan? And suppose you tried to take on the role of Patriarch, would anyone take you seriously? And even if you showed a great deal of insight, wisdom and competence, wouldn't others in the family resent and resist your taking on that role simply because of your youth? Of course!

My point to all of this is this: We are all biologically programmed to play certain roles at certain times in our lives. Society has adjusted itself to accommodate those roles. If we are not biologically prepared, we cannot hope to take on those roles. Indeed, we generally have no inclination or comprehension of the nature of that role. All too often, those who are of the appropriate age and biological status STILL haven't reached the required emotional and mental level of development to take on the role successfully. This is where initiation comes into the picture. Not even a wolf, child of nature and instinct that he might be, simply grows up to be a wolf, he must be MADE a wolf by his community. Take a wolf as a pup and raise him in a domestic, human environment, feed him Alpo from a can, make a pet of him and when he is an adult, he is just a big, dangerous dog! He may be able to kill things, but does he know how to hunt? Does he know how to behave himself in Wolf Society? Can he be returned to the Wild with any real chance of success or even survival? Generally, NO. The same, of course, is true of many animals taken from the Wild as infants. Complex as human beings are, complex as human society is, how on earth can anyone imagine that a male can just grow up to take his place and play his role in society just by having grown up in it? So let me ask you: How can you possibly imagine that you know what the world is all about, how can you begin to think you know how to live, when you have never had any REAL Initiation? How can you be sure you even see the world as it truly is unless you see it through the lens of Initiation? Remember, there was a time when you thought girls were "yucky!"

Let's talk about dogs. As any biologist will confirm, a dog is the result of selective breeding; a dog is a domesticated wolf. We now know that dogs are the result of arrested development. In the selective breeding process, the traits that are arrived at carry the consequence of trapping the animal at a specific stage of biological development; all dogs are by nature ADOLESCENTS. No dog, no matter what his breed, can ever be truly mature, he would be a WOLF. Do you know why dogs bark? Because they are adolescent wolves. Adult wolves don't bark. Do you know what a bark is? It is a totally ambiguous behavior designed primarily to draw attention to oneself, the way a hungry or frustrated puppy does. I once observed a dog inside a fenced yard barking furiously at another dog trotting along the fence line. The outside dog paid absolutely no attention until the inside dog stopped barking and uttered a low growl, then the outside dog jerked his head up, glanced at the inside dog and jumped away from the fence.

There are two kinds of "dogs" in this world, lost dogs and yard dogs. The lost dog is the lucky one; lost dogs can be found, yard dogs don't even know they're lost! The sorry fact is, all uninitiated adult human males are adolescents.

Secularists who say spanking is wrong, the death penalty is bad and that abortion is okay (etc., etc.) are calling God a liar!

Myths are symbols, archetypes and coded messages. Do you know what Dragons symbolize? "Time", time is the ultimate enemy of human beings and the destroyer of our hopes and ideals. That's why virgins were always being gobbled up by dragons in mythical tales; sooner or later, time gobbles up virginity. Of course we all know that "time is money", which is why dragons always sleep on a pile of gold.

Stop trying to be happy by getting things. You can just as easily learn to be happy by getting rid of things. Better yet, shift your attachment to broader things, such as the Glory of God's Creation; learn to exult in the majesty of the moment and place, after all…it belongs to you as much as anyone. The Order of the Hunt was never designed to save your soul, but it might just save your "life".

There's an old saying, "Once you know how to ask the question, it will answer itself." The problem is that you may never arrive at even a rudimentary form of the question. That's what Tricksters are for…not to feed you the question or the answer, but to provoke you into formulating and asking the question and asking it aright. He may even have to trick you into asking it, but YOU have to ask. An answer means nothing unless you have asked the question. Remember poor Parsifal?

Gaston Phebus, author of the medieval "Book of the Hunt", was held to be the highest authority on hunting in the 14th century. Jean Froissart, the great chronicler of chivalry, called Phebus, "The embodiment of the Chivalric Ideal." You may ask, "Why is he the embodiment of Chivalry just because he is the leading authority on The Hunt?" Anyone of the 14th century could answer that question for you: "Who else would be more qualified? As The King judges the people, so the Huntsman judges The King!"

That the King is indeed subject to the Huntsman's authority is illustrated by Sir Francis Bacon's statement that Forests and hunting are the King's prerogative and the FIRST marks of Honor and Nobility, and the ornament of a flourishing kingdom. So, while not officially admitted, the Huntsman was the First Citizen of the Kingdom, the True Arbiter of who was worthy of any position in society. No one can be a part of Nature unless he takes part in Nature.

You can't win against a blind man in the dark. He is in his element and you are not. God has given the blind man an acute sense of hearing; all his senses are sharpened. The blind man hears what you cannot, and understands what he hears. In like manner, the man who is wounded in the right leg also receives certain gifts to compensate for his injured limb. Perhaps he does not know it, perhaps nothing has happened to trigger his compensatory power, or, for whatever reason, he is uninitiated and cannot access that power.

I have never been able to find those Scriptures which justify, demand or permit a Christian Man to be a wimp! Where are they?

What is Honor? I will tell you first what it is not. It is not what we receive. It is not an award, a medal, applause or admiration. It is not something we can demand, we can only COMMAND respect and Honor. Honor is not the grudging deference of a yes-man hoping to gain some reward or advantage. It is not the cowering obedience of weaklings. Honor is not the due of strutting, arrogant, intimidating pretenders. Honor is what we live by; it is implementing the highest moral principles in one's own life and character. Honor is strength with humility, authority with courtesy, justice with wisdom, dignity without pride, and mercy without indulgence.

A True Man of Honor must never show anger. Don't even show much concern. Seek the advice of the wise but keep your own counsel. In matters of justice, don't ever think of "teaching someone a lesson". When a matter is to be dealt with, plan it, leaving nothing to chance, then expedite that plan efficiently and judiciously, without anger or bravado.

Perhaps someone will say, "Just because the Huntsman was the First Citizen of society in the middle ages, doesn't make him the Arbiter of anything today, times change."

From the standpoint of arbitrary law and jurisprudence, this might seem like a valid argument, on the other hand, the Huntsman's position and duty in society was never a formal, LEGAL situation, it arose naturally, it is a genetic imperative, a Divine Mandate if you will. Thus it has never been rescinded and cannot be rescinded. The Hunter is the basic "program" of our genes, and it's never going to go away. The militarist is a usurper, the Politician is a usurper, the power of wealth and influence is usurpation of authority. As I've said before, our power and authority may be eclipsed, but it is not diminished.

Life is not about what happens to you, it's about how you respond to what happens to you. Accident, illness, injustice, tragedy, or fame and fortune…it's all SCHOOL. It's all about opportunities to choose, to decide, to grow, to develop Character…or not!

All authority comes from above. Jesus taught this, the Roman soldier who came to Jesus to ask Him to heal his servant knew this. It has always been so, and always will be so. Every governmental authority is granted whatever authority he has from someone above him. Ultimate authority comes from God Himself. If God commands, only a fool disobeys. Any so-called "authority figure" who attempts to seize authority for himself, to countermand the clear requirements which God has set forth for man, has violated the very basis of his office and should be dismissed, prosecuted and punished. Under our present system, the actions of Phineas may seem like vigilante justice, but God approved his intervention.

In my opinion (and I am an Elder over fifty years of age) any man in his right mind, who acts according to clear understanding of God's commandments and without any ulterior motives, with a clear conscience, MUST act when it is evident that those assigned to positions of authority cannot or will not act. Indeed, such a man has an absolute moral obligation to act...to stand quietly by is evil. The Bible states clearly the old axiom that to witness a crime and not act, is to be guilty of that crime.

The conscience, what is it? It is an open wound between the soul of man and the Spirit of God. It is a wound shared in common by that man and God. It is the very wound of Christ which pains us...though only distantly...because it pains God when we sin and can only be soothed by virtue.

This wound is the door by which the Holy Spirit enters into the heart of man to dwell there. Yes, pagans and atheists may have a conscience of sorts, because the wound is there. The door is open, standing open as a witness against them, for the Spirit has not been invited to come in, and perhaps is not welcome.

Saint Paul speaks of those whose conscience has been seared by a hot iron. He describes the custom of cauterizing an open wound with fire so that it ceases to bleed. The wound is thus closed and gradually heals over with tough scar tissue with no feeling in it.

Here's an object lesson for you. The Bible often speaks of leprosy and Christ often healed lepers. Do you know what lepers die of? Leprosy doesn't kill you, leprosy only makes you impervious to pain, consequently the leper tends to ignore little injuries. The lack of pain makes him careless, he becomes subject to frequent injuries and, because there is no pain, he ignores them. These little injuries can become infected resulting in the loss of a finger, a hand, a nose or ear. Even large injuries aren't felt and are given minimal care. The leper dies by attrition, not from the disease, but because he has ceased to FEEL.

As the wounds of Christ are the portal of conscience and thus of Grace between God and man, I sometimes think that in like manner, the wound of the Anwalt is the portal between men through which

Honor is implanted in the heart of the initiate. The open wound is an open doorway through which, by the principle of mystical contagion, all the qualities of True Manhood flow from one man to another.

So long as the initiate doesn't wholly reject that wound, the cup of Honor will continue to fill to overflowing. The initiate can never fail to have received the gift, for while a man's word may be falsely or lightly given by either party, there is no lying or lack of Truth and sincerity in Blood. Even one who spills his blood with false intent has ensnared himself, for he is bound by his deed before God and man by the very presence of that blood. Blood is the answer to every question, the solution to every problem, the bond of every covenant. Is it any wonder that the myth of the Spear of Longinus was such a potent symbol in the middle ages? The wounds of Christ are the True Penumbra...the way between worlds.

BRINKSMANSHIP. I don't know anyone who has ever done the Fifth Initiation...which I do not recommend...but we all understand that it confers great powers. What most young and/or new initiates don't know...and aren't told, is that the first four initiations also confer great powers. Because of the nature of these powers (and human nature being what it is), they generally aren't told...at least not right away. There's always the question of whether to tell them, what to tell them and when to tell them. Can they be trusted? Or will they just get themselves into trouble?

As it happens, the initiation process matures a man, this instills a certain degree of reserve and conservatism. This, in turn (ironically) tends to prevent them from discovering their new talents. It is only gradually, as they come to gain more wisdom and insight, experience and skill, that they come to any awareness of what they have. Even when circumstances force them into situations that might spontaneously trigger one of these powers, they generally assume it was coincidence or "dumb luck" that saw them through. A few will wonder if it was something else, a fraction of those will suspect it was something more extraordinary, but still won't realize what it was.

One of these powers is Brinksmanship. The Old Brothers called a man who exercised this power a "Rander" (another one of those many names and titles which we have heaped to ourselves over the centuries). Rander means a "Borderer", not in the sense of a frontiersman, as in English, but one who "lives on the edge", and knows how to live on the edge.

The "edge" is where things happen, circumstances can be changed, decisive events occur. Look up brinksmanship in the dictionary, it'll tell you it refers to one who understands the art and practice of pressing dangerous situations to the limit of safety before stopping. Well, Webster's got it wrong this time. A Brinksman (in our Tradition) is one who understands the art and practice of pressing dangerous situations to the limit in order to win! Our Tradition makes a lot of references to the edge of things, the place where one thing becomes another. We understand how powerful these places are and how they relate to Brinkmanship. It's all about power and authority.

It's not unlike a policeman. He goes through training and comes out with a badge and a gun. The badge gives him authority, The gun gives him power. He can enforce the law with a gun, but it is extremely likely to cause him a lot of grief if he doesn't have a badge to go with it. If he has a badge and no gun, he can try to enforce the law, but that can create even bigger problems. In the initiation process you get both the badge and the gun, but no one tells you about it.

A man can readily understand authority and will soon come to feel it and exercise it, but that mystical "gun" isn't so readily seen. This new talent is a purely instinctual skill that is operated on a subconscious level and understood only by the subconscious. Our common vernacular uses the term, "having an edge", meaning to have an advantage. The expression arises from our subconscious knowledge of Brinksmanship (whether we're capable of accessing it or not).

Have you ever seen one of those old B-western movies? Many of them used the fist-fight on the cliff to add tension to the story. The "cliff-hanger" was an archetypal event which the subconscious recognizes, and no matter how often you see it performed…even in watching the same movie a second or third time…it never fails to elicit the instinctual gut-tightening reaction.

In any situation, against any opponent, the Huntsman has the edge. The Huntsman knows where the cliff is and can stampede the buffalo over it. The Huntsman knows where the cliff is in the dark and can maneuver his opponent toward the edge. The Huntsman is in no real danger, just the "bad guy"…always and only! The edge is the Huntsman's best weapon. Even when he seems to lose, he wins, because he has the AUTHORITY (the moral high-ground) on his side. A loss is only a staging point for a huge come-back, or the door to an even greater opportunity. Mystical nonsense? Try it and see!

What I'm describing is not inflated self-confidence arising from some false sense of superiority. It isn't courage drawn from having found meaning and purpose in one's life through the initiation process. In no way is it simply "the power of positive thinking". The initiation process actually frees your instincts and intuition so that you "know" where the brink is, and understand that the brink is your best weapon. Your opponent doesn't know where the brink is and will either refuse to follow you to the edge, or won't even suspect there is an edge to fall off of.

Just like in the movies, the hero has dispatched the bad guy and yet is free of any moral responsibility. The hero didn't kill the bad guy…he fell! The edge kills the bad guy! He had a choice; all he had to do was not pursue the hero. Another interesting moral point is that the bad guy is defacto "bad" or else he would surely have "bravely run away". Only motives of greed, stupidity, dishonor, hatred (or any other unrighteous motive) can keep you from seeing the edge.

Don't misunderstand, one doesn't have to be morally "perfect" in order to win, you just have to be "right". Does this mean you will always win? No, but your ratio of "wins" to "losses" will skyrocket, and even your losses will become clear opportunities to correct and refine your character so that your future success ratio increases still more.

So, how is Brinkmanship conferred? It's just like riding a bicycle; you can't learn it from a book or work it out intellectually, but a shove in the right direction gets you started. If your sense of balance is intact, you'll teach yourself in a matter of moments and never forget. Brinksmanship is an intense perception of environment and options, the very talent every good hunter needs and develops...only more so. Clues so faint or subtle that they don't even register on the conscious mind are picked up and processed on the deepest, most primitive levels of the brain. Insights and probabilities are computed and conclusions, tactics and courses of action are developed, then flashed to the conscious mind as urges, reflex actions and hunches. Add to this a dash of genuine extra-sensory perception, and you have the makings of a natural-born killer, a talented artist, a razor sharp negotiator, a great philosopher or an Olympic athlete. How often the Brinksmanship instinct kicks in and how powerful it is will depend on your commitment, intensity of need, how well it's cultivated and how much you trust it.

One of the reasons an initiate doesn't seem to know he has it until he needs it is that it isn't at all intrusive; it doesn't provoke or inspire one to do dangerous things, it simply leads the way if you need to go there, and will pay attention.

The first initiation confers the freedom to act. The second initiation gives one the power to act. The third initiation gives the authority to act. The fourth initiation gives one the freedom from the need to act.

Tending the fire, the Denkmal and the Repose seem to be support systems for the various initiations and provide reinforcement...sort of a "booster shot".

I'm reminded of a story I read once about a Viking boy who was assigned the task of tending the fire. He became very attached to his task, so much so that people began to think he was feeble minded. He talked almost not at all, cared nothing for playing with the other boys, had no interest in hunting, riding horses, playing games or learning much of anything. His father became angry and wanted to foster him out to a strict disciplinarian, or punish him in some way to get him to wake up to his other responsibilities, but the Elders urged him to leave the boy alone…they knew the value of tending the fire. Then, one day when all the men were away, the farmstead was attacked by outlaws. Instantly the boy, now about eighteen years old, sprang up, grabbed a sword from the wall and slew all the outlaws. He had become a full-fledged warrior and a master swordsman. This is an initiation tale.

So what about the fifth initiation (which I do not recommend)? I can't really say. I suspect that it confers all of the above named skills in MASSIVE proportions. It may do something totally different, all I know about it is hints and rumors.

Everywhere I turn, everything I read, all my research reveals time and again that the Huntsman is somehow connected to the black-smith. Scholars in mythology and the rules of correspondences, say that the Trickster archetype is common to both the Hunter and the Craftsman. I'm sorry to say, but the Trickster is even pressed into duty as the patron of merchants, too! I've come to suspect that the harbin-gers of technology and commerce are the "dark side" of the hunter psyche. Perhaps this is why we are warned to beware the god-who-limps. This is a reference to Hephaestus, the Greek god of fire and metal-working who had an injured leg (we'll hope it was his LEFT leg!). The warning applies to all forms of technology, commerce and industry. As you can see, even the Greeks knew that the god of tech-nology had an inherent defect and weakness.

As I said, every culture in every time and place seems to link the Hunter with the Blacksmith. I've only recently learned that even the Rechabites of Israel were somehow related to the Kenites who were nomadic blacksmiths and metal-workers. There's a puzzle here.

One may well ask, how is it that the hunting orders so greatly despise cities and consider them evil and a source of corruption? Scripture plainly speaks of "the New Jerusalem", "The City of God" and other such references. If cities are intrinsically evil, why would God promise us a "Heavenly City"?

The answer may not be obvious, but it is simple: Recall the Scripture verse which says, "Unless the Lord builds the house, they labor in vain who build it." God never told men to build cities, they took it upon themselves. Only God knows how to build a city properly, leave it to Him.

How is it that the church rejects **conversion by the sword** and calls it wrong? This was exactly how the Faith was spread in ancient times! Missionaries called upon the King to accept the new doctrine. The King's family and household members were almost always the first converts. Once the king accepted Christianity, he issued a decree that all of his subjects must also be Baptized. The first generation may well have been Christians in name only, but they soon grew to believe truly, and subsequent generations were BORN into the Faith. So it happened all over Europe, and even the Roman Empire rushed to the baptismal font once Constantine endorsed the Christian religion. Those nations which didn't come into the Church in this manner usually had the Faith thrust upon them by invading Crusaders. Jesus said, "Upon this rock I will build my Church, and the gates of hell shall not prevail against it." We seem to forget that the "gates of hell" aren't mobile; they don't go anyplace or attack anybody. Gates are set in a wall and locked to keep others out. It seems obvious to me that Jesus was saying that the Church would attack hell itself and the gates of hell would not be able to stand up against our attack…but we'll never know unless we ATTACK!

Chivalry itself, the very code of honor by which kings were expected to live and the rule of conduct for every nobleman and gentleman alike, was the direct outgrowth of the Rules of the Hunt: To give an animal a sporting chance, to make a kill quick and clean, to never leave a wounded quarry to die a slow and lingering death, to always respect the life of the beast. Those who attack and defame the Hunt attack the very foundation of masculinity itself. They knowingly reject the code of Chivalry and Honor. That is the real reason they oppose hunting.

Jesus called His Disciples to be "Fishers of Men". Only a few of them were actually fishermen. In like manner, one need not be an actual hunter in order to be a True Huntsman.

In both the Gospels of Matthew and Luke, Jesus speaks of the last days saying, "Where the body is the eagles will gather." Eagles are quite obviously known for their hunting skill. Eagles may even be seen as an obvious transition from "fishing" to "hunting". Surely you've seen nature films where an eagle swoops down upon an unsuspecting salmon, snatches it up out of the water and glides off into the heavens with the poor fish clutched in his talons. And Luke also quotes Christ as pointing to the Raven as one who neither sows nor reaps, neither does he own a barn, yet God feeds him.

The Book of Revelation describes the four creatures surrounding the throne of God. The last of the four is "like an Eagle flying". If we take the sequence to have relevance to the ages or stages of God's work, we may conclude that the Eagle comes last…the final phase of God's plan. A brief study of references to Eagles and Ravens in the Bible may provide you with a good deal of food for thought.

Does anyone remember "HIGHER SOURCE"; those 39 people out in California who committed mass suicide a few years ago? We feel sorry for them. We think they were brainwashed. But wait a minute! These were not ignorant, backward, under-privileged people. They were professionals; highly trained individuals who created top-notch, state of the art computer web sites, earning up to $40,000 per assignment. They had a belief system to which they had given absolute loyalty. Do you realize how wonderful that is? They had purpose, life had meaning for them, a cause worth dying for. They had values which meant more to them than life itself! They were "Loyal unto death". You…without such a cause…will die anyway, but it may be a straw death, a death without meaning or purpose; simply the end of your life. Who wants to die as just the final pointless event in a pointless life? If you don't have something worth dying for, you don't have anything worth living for!

Those people didn't have a cause to fight for, or even an "enemy" to resist. They killed themselves as a positive, forward-looking act. They weren't down-trodden, they just had a hope of a better existence on another planet, and they were willing to give up their present luxury accommodations for it.

How has our society failed to elicit that kind of loyalty? How have we failed to command that kind of devotion and service? They may have been "brainwashed", but imagine how happy they were! They didn't live in squalor here on earth, they had lots of money. I recall reporters on the scene describing how immaculately clean and tidy everyone was. These people weren't walking around in some sort of hypnotic zombie trance, they weren't in a drug-induced fog. They were wide awake and articulate.

What they were was COMMITTED! What we call "brainwashed" may have been nothing less than CONVINCED.

Sometimes freedom to choose is no choice at all. What good is freedom of choice if society decides what those choices will be? And when I say "society", I mean "social engineers", market analysts, government bureaucrats and the like. The freedom to choose is a farce when the game has been rigged from the start. Society has already devalued all real choices; they have ridiculed, outlawed, suppressed or eliminated all real choice. What we're faced with is just another kind of mind-control. It keeps us weak and docile and domesticated. We're like cattle milling around in random order. Those who "ride herd on us" are afraid of what might happen if we ever got pointed in the same direction and started moving in unison, or if even an individual got headed off in his own direction. They might lose control. Oh my!

Make no mistake, we are considered a resource, just like a herd of cattle, and those "cowboys" in Washington, the Pentagon and Madison Avenue don't want you to have any real control in your life. That's why they keep you diverted, entertained, off balance with one national crisis after another. If YOU had a plan, a cause, a goal, and they couldn't turn it to their own use, they would get real stressed-out. They might have to arrest you, shoot you, lock you away someplace…for your own good.

I really don't like using a suicide cult as an example of freedom of choice, but it illustrates the point so well; they were willing to die to get out of this society. Wide awake people are driven to anger, grief, or despair in a meaningless life.

My whole purpose in mentioning "cults" is to point out how desperate many people are to escape a world that offers every material opportunity but is utterly devoid of any real spiritual benefit. Why wouldn't the early Christians sometimes OFFER themselves for martyrdom? The real question is why modern Christians don't!

God forbid that anyone should ever label a Hunting Order as a brainwashing cult. Hunters are the very opposite of a cult; we tend to be extremely self-reliant, solitary and contented individuals. No man is ever sworn to obey or serve the Order or any member of the Order. The initiate is expected only to pledge himself to the highest moral principles of Christian life and to conduct himself at all times as a Man of Honor. Indeed, he is not even required to associate with other Brothers after his initiation, attend meetings or participate in our activities. Huntsmen are, by nature, solitary men. Only God is the Huntsman's Master. He should associate with Christians, attend Church, be in service to his community. If he wishes to "hang out" with Brothers of the Hunt, that's entirely up to him. And no Brother should ever be questioned, ridiculed, shunned or imposed upon in any way for failing to "run with the pack". It is the duty of the Order to initiate men into the Life of Honor, not try to live it for him! Who knows what his vocation may be, perhaps it is exactly God's will that he should depart from our ranks. Certainly we must try to determine and be sure that he has not been inadvertently offended or alienated in some way, and to make amends if necessary, but beyond that, he is a sovereign entity owing allegiance only to God.

As Sir Francis Bacon said, The Hunt is the first marks of Nobility and Honor. But who is qualified to determine that those marks are present and operative in a "king"? Only a Huntsman. And how does a Huntsman arrive at this high status? By initiation into a Hunting Order. What, can no official government entity certify, recognized or swear him into office? Why should they? Not even the priests of Israel were "sworn in", they took no "oath of office", they were priests by right of primogeniture. In the tale of Tristan and Isolde, Tristan arrives on the scene with absolutely no credentials; his knowledge of the proper way to conduct a Hunt and to field dress a deer were taken as the marks of true nobility. On this evidence alone, King Mark accepted him at his court. Tristan didn't have to present letters of recommendation or a government I.D. Neither was he questioned about the latest fashion, diplomatic gossip or his parentage. He didn't have to display any social refinements other than his authority as a good Huntsman.

If the king is unworthy, certainly those subordinate to him are unworthy. The only way to restore everyone's Honor is to depose the unworthy "king".

In a formal Hunt, only the Huntsman and the Master of the hunt are permitted to kill the quarry. This alone shows that the Huntsman is equal to the King. That the Huntsman acts as absolute arbiter of the Hunt shows that he is the King's Superior.

Should the Master of the Hunt violate the rules of the Hunt, that is to say, if he has acted rashly, with cruelty, anger, a lack of discretion, courtesy or respect; if he acted in any way incompetently or dishonorable, the Huntsman might declare the quarry an "unworthy kill". This would deny the Master of the Hunt the right to deliver the coup de grace, and the Huntsman would either let the animal go or dispatch it himself. Of course the Huntsman's decision was NEVER challenged or questioned, but his intention could be easily read. Members of the court were experienced hunters who could see that a stag, boar, wolf or bear was a worthy quarry. They could also recognize that it was the king himself, by his unworthy behavior, that made the kill unworthy. So, to declare a kill unworthy might mark the king as unworthy rather than the beast.

May I also add that a "king" need not engage in the Hunt under the authority of a Huntsman in order to be declared unworthy by that Huntsman. An experienced Huntsman recognizes the traits of unworthiness even in those who do not hunt.

Hunting Orders are a part of that great and hallowed body or ethics and morals which stands above and behind statute law and lends authority to statute law. It is that great rule of jurisprudence known as "The Unwritten Law". As surely as you are born in this country, you are a Citizen of this country. You receive your Citizenship by birth. By birth you have the right to become a Huntsman; a few thousand years of agrarian society simply cannot even begin to erase the millennia of genetic natural selection that has infused your very nature with the hunting instinct. It is a biological imperative. Even science now tells us that blood type is an indicator of one's genetic predisposition to hunting. Blood type "O" is the blood of the natural-born hunter. Other blood types are very late developments which explains why they are decidedly less common than type "O".

Laws that really mean anything in the universal sense, arise out of the Morality of Natural Consequence and, as such, don't even need to be written down. This, of course, is the entire foundation of the Constitution of the United States of America; "We hold these Truths to be self-evident…" not needing any authority or explanation beyond their existence. Such Truths are so natural and evident that they need no formal enactment. Our very instincts tell us it is against "The Law" to dump human fetuses in an open field and attempt to set them on fire. That's why an abortionist in Oklahoma was arrested when he dumped two hundred unborn babies and tried to burn them. Unfortunately, because such an inhuman act was considered too horrible to contemplate, no such statute was on the books, and because our courts are only allowed to rule on statute law, the abortionist went free. Did that mean he was innocent of a crime? If so, then why did he try to HIDE his actions? He knew very well that he was committing a CRIME. Should he have been punished? Of course! And when people say, "Someone should do something!" We, the Hunting Orders, are that very "Someone".

It is obvious that much of what I say sounds as if I'm laying the ground-work for a political movement or a political revolution. In fact, I'm saying absolutely nothing of the kind. By demonstrating that the Huntsman is the Highest Authority in the Realm and the First Citizen of the Realm, I am establishing all my lesser claims as being equally valid; that the Hunting Orders are a natural, necessary and authoritative resource for the stability and health of society and individuals within society.

Answer these two questions and remember those answers. If you could be any animal, bird or fish, what would you choose? Now, if you REALLY WERE an animal, bird or fish, what would it be? This will give you some real insights into your own Character and aspirations.

When Prince Albert died, Queen Victoria of England was inconsolable. No member of her family, household, ministers at court or the

Royal Physician could prevail upon her to pull herself out of her depression, after all…she was the Queen, who could command her to do anything she didn't wish to do? So, what did they do? They sent to Scotland and summoned Prince Albert's Royal Huntsman! He and only he could prevail upon the Queen. It was he and only he that she would obey.

In the story of Snow White, how is it established succinctly by the story teller that the evil queen was truly evil and not acting from "royal prerogative"? By the fact that the evil queen ordered the Loyal Huntsman to murder Snow White and he, instead of obeying her orders, urged Snow White to escape. In an age when royalty had such prerogatives, such a device was helpful in assuring one's audience that the person being described was indeed acting by evil intent and not from any political necessity.

Jesus Christ commissioned His followers to preach the Gospel. He also commanded them to denounce the unworthy. Matt. 10:13-14.

If Holy Scripture gives us ants, doves and serpents as examples of wise behavior, why would we ignore God when He also pointed to Ravens as examples of virtue and trust?

I'm not familiar with laws in other states, but in my own state it is illegal for an emergency vehicle to exceed the speed limit when responding to a call. But whenever a house is on fire or a 911 call comes in for a cardiac arrest, no one will thank you for observing a 20mph speed limit in getting to the scene. Sometimes common sense (that "Unwritten Law" I mentioned earlier) simply overrides "law".

Archaeological evidence tells us that agriculture only began about twelve thousand years ago. This same evidence tells us that wars (organized, systematic aggression) also began at exactly the same time. Before the agrarian age, the concept of war was unknown. Without doubt there were instances of murder (although we have no tangible evidence of it), but war arose in direct response to tribes living in fixed communities and producing a surplus of food. Failed crops and the all too human desire to get something for nothing coupled with the threat of starvation and perhaps another tribe's refusal to share or trade, sent war parties to "liberate" the other tribe's food stores. Matriarchy (if indeed any such system ever actually existed) was a very brief transitional stage between hunter/gatherer cultures and agrarian/military cultures.

All evidence confirms that hunting cultures were extraordinarily friendly and generous. When you want to kill a mammoth, you'll take all the help you can get. Dressing out a mammoth also required all possible help. Hunting parties almost certainly welcomed an encounter with another hunting party and shared the work and the meat fairly. Evidence also shows that they had designated rendevous sites where they met on a regular basis, probably to share hunting lore, learn where certain herds and resources might be located, to trade goods, meet potential mates, initiate the young, and perform various hunting and religious rites. Friendship and generosity are still the traits of a hunter.

There is a certain self-proclaimed authority on the initiation process who actually tries to discredit initiation, saying that because we no longer live in a hunter/gatherer society, initiation is worthless. He insists that because we don't have a uniform culture, we can't have a "universal" initiation process. He feels that if all we did was hunt bears or go fishing, initiation would work, but because some men are taxi drivers while others are brain surgeons, rites of passage have no relevance. He appears to be stuck in the feminist mindset which only thinks in terms of protecting, providing and procreation. Of course, there is nothing wrong in these things either, and initiation encompasses these very real areas of life. He fails to recognize that the whole foundation of any culture lies in HONOR. Never confuse a job with a vocation! In the course of a man's life, he may be a taxi driver, a lumberjack and a brain surgeon, but just as the money he gets for each of those jobs is the same, the sense of honor, responsibility and integrity needed in each field of endeavor is exactly the same. Jobs make money and money pays the bills, the real crux of the matter is Honor. Hunting initiations aren't centered on hunting bears or programming computers, it's centered on loyalty, commitment and Honor. A man who is consistent within himself is happy with his life and a valued member of society.

One day Jesus of Nazareth was walking by the sea of Galilee where he saw two fishermen, James and John, with their father, Zebedee, mending nets. Jesus called these two young men to follow him and become "fishers of men". He calls them, "Sons of Thunder". Now imagine that scene. Here's an old man mending nets with his two sons, tending to their family business of being fishermen when along comes an itinerant preacher to lure his sons away from their work, leaving the old man to fend for himself. Can you imagine Zebedee shaking his fist and "thundering" at them as they walk away? Can you imagine Jesus breaking the tension by saying, "I'll call you boys 'the Sons of Thunder'".

Now imagine a story that Jesus told about a man walking around with a two-by-four stuck in his own eye offering to help a friend who only has a speck of sawdust in his eye. Visualize that scene and try to imagine what a funny picture that presented to His audience. It must have been hilarious. These are Trickster traits. And, as I've said before, why would the God of the Universe who designed all the archetypes, not use them to full advantage? And the Grandfather of all archetypes is the Trickster.

In virtually all cultures, the Trickster is the messenger of the gods (or GOD). The Trickster often makes paradoxical statements and gives ambivalent answers to questions. He often answers a question with a question. He uses entertaining and humorous stories to illustrate his message or to teach a principle. The Trickster is famous for encountering a circumstance that is stuck in the status quo and introducing an element of disruption in order to shake up the people and circumstances with the intention of making them better. He often teaches with riddles and evades direct questions altogether. He contradicts accepted "truths". He makes men look like fools in order to make them wise. He uses shock tactics, irony, surprise and object lessons to get his message across. He is often accused of being irreverent by current standards, even blasphemous. He does the unexpected, even the impossible. He may even hide or withhold his true identity at times to accomplish his goals. He is especially thought to hang out with people of questionable or unsavory character.

All of these traits are classic Trickster characteristics, they also define the personality of the Son of God, Jesus Christ.

I have a couple of tests for you. First, draw a picture of a tree. DO IT! Don't read another word until you've drawn a picture of a tree! Now put it aside and do the next test.

In this test, I want you to draw a square, a circle, a triangle and an octagon (you know, like a stop sign). Try not to think about it too much…just pick the one you "like best" and write the number "1" in it. Pick the one you like best of the three remaining and write the number "2". Then do "3" and "4". Okay, did you do it? If not, you're only cheating yourself. These tests can only be done ONCE IN A LIFE-TIME! If you know the answers in advance, the tests are totally invalid.

That tree you drew, mentally divide the tree right down the center. The left side of the tree is your mother, the right side is your father. Does the tree lean more to one side than the other? Is it more full or more detailed on one side than the other? Do limbs seem to reach or struggle toward one side or the other? This will tell you where your sympathies and identity does or does not lie. Is there a ground line? Are the roots visible? How broad the base of the tree is says how well "grounded" you are, how rooted you are. Visible roots speak of a connection with your extended family, ancestors or ethnic origin. Flowers and grass at the base of the tree disclose an optimistic outlook; an interest in family and friends. Birds, squirrels and the like in or around a tree also speaks of fecundity, sociability and optimism.

How much shading did you put into the tree trunk and limbs? Is it more shaded on one side than the other? This suggests an unhappy childhood or a bad relationship with one or both parents.

Are there any cut-off limbs on the tree trunk? Are there any knot-holes or other anomalies on the trunk? These reflect traumas in your childhood, either physical or emotional. To demonstrate the truth of this, think back to any such possible event. How old were you? Now measure the position of the knothole or squiggle. If you're currently 28 years old and the blemish is half way up the trunk, it suggests you were 14 years old when it happened. It's easy to do, and very accurate. It may have been a fall from your bicycle or the divorce or death of a parent. The size of the knothole and how detailed or black it is says how traumatic it was.

The tree's foliage is pretty much "where your head is now". Is the foliage detailed or is it sparse, scanty, lots of bare limbs? You haven't reached your potential in life. Is it vague, sketchy, sort of a general suggestion of leaves and limbs? You are a bit nebulous and probably have no real ambition. No leaves at all? You are depressed, feeling like a failure. Is the foliage more apparent on one side or the other? Your goals, dreams, ambitions, education, all are slanted toward one of your parents.

Use your imagination, the tree is a portrait of you and it's true.

The four geometric symbols you drew. The one you like best is your dominate interest, everything else is subordinate to that interest. Any effort you put into number "4" is to further goals relevant to number "1". The same applies in a descending order. Your whole life may seem to focus on number "2" or "3", but it is secretly to gain the advantage in number "1". Got the idea? Okay, here it is: The square symbolizes security; emotional, financial, physical or whatever. The circle is sex. Plain and simple. The triangle is intellectual interests. And the octagon represents patience. I'll leave you to ponder the relevance of each to the others.

I feel certain that these two tests, and a third test, which I will describe next, are recent additions to our Tradition. I have never been able to find these in any psychological text books (although I'm sure they must be there, somewhere). One psychologist friend of mine was very intrigued by the "tree" and seemed genuinely astounded that it worked so well, and admitted that he had never heard of it either. But I still can't really imagine the Old Brothers having such resources at their disposal.

The value of these tests seems to be a chance to document, if you will, where you are in life, with yourself, your level of maturity, and maybe to help define special problem areas. It is undoubtedly an excellent way of gauging the rate and state of maturity that follows the initiation process, as well.

THE ROAD OF LIFE. This is the third test. You will need pencil and paper again. STOP RIGHT NOW! Do the test before reading the explanation. OKAY? Okay!

Take as much time as you like and jot down as many details as seems necessary. Don't attempt to remember what you were thinking…write it all down first and completely.

First, imagine you are walking down a country road. Whatever that means to you, fix it clearly in your mind. Now, describe it in as much detail as you like.

Secondly, imagine, as you walk along, you approach a house on the right hand side of the road. Describe the house in as much detail as you like.

Third. As you continue on down the road, you find a key lying in the road. Describe the key and what you do with it.

Fourth. As you continue on down the road, you encounter a bear. Describe the bear and what you do.

Fifth. As you walk along, you come to a body of water. Describe the body of water and how you get to the other side. NOTE: You can't go around it, you must cross it.

Sixth. Continuing along the road, you come to a wall. Again, you cannot go around this wall. Describe the wall and how you get to the other side.

Seventh, and last. What do you find on the other side?

I recommend that this test be administered to those at least 21 years old. NEVER, EVER give the test to anyone under age 14. Remember, it can only be taken once in a lifetime.

If you have completed the test, write the date on it, sign it...and pass it to the front of the class. Oh, sorry, I forgot! Ready? Here we go!

The road you were on is your life as you perceive it. That's not to say it is really that way, only how YOU perceive your life. People who have rotten lives sometimes romanticize them, or simply don't respond to circumstances the way someone else might. If it was a sweet spring day, fluffy clouds in the sky, the sun is shining, you're barefooted and wiggling your toes in soft, cool dirt as gentle breezes play in your hair, you like your life, or at least have adapted to it happily. If it is a cold, dark day, a hot, sweaty day, the road is hard, full of ruts and rocks, narrow and straight or rugged and hilly, you are not a happy camper.

Was there a fence on one side, both sides? Was it a barbed wire fence or a rail fence? Were there pastures with black and white cows or a deer grazing? Were there trees in the distance? Fences equal restrictions. Cattle are symbols of peace. A deer might mean adventure or spiritual concepts. A fence on the left is a restraint created by your mother. On the right, a fence is something your father did that holds you back. As before, use your imagination. It works.

The house you found is your mother. (Don't ask me why it was on the RIGHT side of the road, nobody told me and I failed to ask). A large, white, antebellum house with high white columns out front suggests a mother who was rigid and formal; just a bit too matronly, too proper, too imposing. A cozy cottage with a big front porch, lots of flowers and fruit trees, a picket fence, smoke coming from the chimney, well that's everyone's ideal mom...could you loan her to me? Porches represent friendly, welcoming qualities, homey and comfortable. Often we can determine how many siblings a man has by how many trees are in the yard, especially if he describes them as fruit trees. One guy described an old shack, red roofed, broken windows, deserted and falling down. He swore it couldn't be his mother, but on closer examination we leaned his mother was an alcoholic who abandoned him, was dying, had no friends...and had red hair. What can I say...it works.

The key is always interesting; it is your education or hopes for education. Guys who find car keys have very material goals. They want to get there fast, too. Very ornate gold keys are golden opportunities. Rusty old antique keys belong to romantic types, dreamers. Skeleton keys are often found; they fit many doors, who knows what doors they may open? Education for the sake of education, to take you who knows where. What you do with the key matters. Some put it in their pocket and walk on. Some put it in their BACK pocket. This suggests they are getting or will get an education even if they don't really know why. Some just drop it back on the ground. They assume it belongs to someone else, not them. One fellow put it in the mailbox in front of the house. Upon questioning him, we learned that he had gotten his higher education by correspondence courses through the mail. He also admitted that he only did it to please his mother.

The bear is interesting; it represents problems and dilemmas in life. How big and bad the bear is, how you react and what happens tells you how you feel about and respond to trouble. Some see a grizzly bear, others may see a tiny bear cub and want to scuffle and play, then swatting it on the rump, send it off into the woods. So, do you freeze up, climb a tree, turn and run, look for a big stick, sneak past, wave your arms, yell and rush at it?

Water is always sex. Was it the Pacific Ocean, a raging mountain stream, a stagnant pond filled with snakes and frogs, a quiet pool? Everyone has a slightly different image. And did you build a raft, find a canoe, build a bridge, roll up your pant legs and wade across (because it was so shallow), did you decide it was a hot day, pull of all your clothes and go swimming for awhile?

And then, there's the wall. The wall is death and how you see it. Some find a low wall made of natural field stone which they can sit down on and swing their legs across. Some find a high prison-type wall, made of concrete or bricks. Some contrive very strange gimmicks and strategies for getting over or through the wall. One fellow found a "key stone", removed it, crawled through, then pulled the stone back in place behind him. One guy found a tree growing near the wall, climbed the tree and, just as he leaped toward the wall, he seemed to realize that he was carrying a heavy backpack which somehow broke loose and fell away as he reached the wall (his physical body, no doubt, since he had some serious health problems which he saw as "burdens"). The more you complicate the wall, the more your denial and fear of death.

And what did you find on the other side? Some see the same road going on, except now, the day seems brighter, the breeze cooler and more refreshing. Many find themselves in a wide, open field overlooking a valley. Some see a village or a "Shining City" in the distance. One individual, I'm sorry to say, simply couldn't imagine anything; just a black void. What you've found, of course, is Life after Death. Some rest, some are invigorated, some travel on, some settle down for a while. Most find it extremely inviting.

Those who study animal behavior have coined a phrase, "innate releasing mechanism" (IRM) to describe the means whereby instinctive behavior sleeping in the animal's genes is awakened in response to a triggering event. As we all know, animals are born with certain instinctual responses; just-hatched turtles scamper directly to the sea. A newborn human infant knows how to nurse. My favorite is that newly hatched chicks will run for cover when they see the shadow of a hawk fly over. They don't respond if the shadow is a pigeon or a duck. Even a stuffed hawk drawn overhead on a wire will startle the chick...unless it is drawn BACKWARDS, in which case the chick is not fooled; hawks don't fly backwards and the instinctive behavior isn't triggered.

Initiation is an "IRM" which human society has discovered as a means to release specific survival oriented behaviors that lie sleeping in our genes. Unless these instincts are released we never fully mature, never completely "wake up" to life, are never adequately prepared for the contingencies of life. Most men, if they are to have these initiating experiences at all, must rely on spontaneous events in life which may or may not occur at all. These triggering experiences may come at the wrong time, in the wrong manner, too late in life, or in some devastating and tragic manner with which they simply cannot cope. This is the advantage of clearly defined initiations conducted in a controlled environment by competent, experience Elders who can coach and reassure the initiate. This isn't hocus-pocus, witchcraft, pop-psychology or brainwashing, it's exactly the same as life-experience, but done symbolically and methodically. What we know is this: The human brain doesn't seem to know the difference between a real event and a symbolic even. Remember, actors playing a part experience the same physiological changes as the characters they play; fear, weeping, increased blood pressure, nausea, disorientation, anger, despair, depression. That's why we are addicted to watching actors play roles, we are trying to absorb their experiences vicariously to make them our own; they are mild initiations...and all too often, the WRONG kind! A good action picture sets us on the edge of our seat, women weep at all the right places in a "chick flick". We know "it's only a movie", but it has an effect, doesn't it? Initiation is all the more powerful because it is "really happening" to US.

"A good fire makes the story dance!" Somehow, firelight enhances a winter's tale. It brings the story to life, static objects and ideas seem to change shape and take on movement in firelight. Firelight seems to be one of the most conducive means to introspection, insight, inspiration, even visionary experiences. There are other things which can accommodate or facilitate such experiences, but firelight actually seems to provoke these states of mind, hence the ancient custom of setting the uninitiated boy to tend the fire.

Now let us speak of things too grievous to be borne, too dark and burdensome to relate, and yet we shall relate them. We shall now consider the Huntsman as a kind of "sin eater"; one who sacrifices for the sake of Honor. We shall speak of the Huntsman in war. Even here the Huntsman was First Among Equals. While each man in war had his duty and task, the Huntsman was expected to bear many roles and bear them the extra mile. The Huntsman was called upon to be the advance scout, the spy, the assassin. He must be adept in the use of many kinds of weapons and tactics, he would set booby-traps, gather intelligence, make maps and create diversions. He must be expert in the use of disguise and subterfuge. He must be hunter, cook, physician, engineer, diplomat and fool as occasion required. He was called upon to train knights in the skills of forest warfare, in ambush and wilderness survival. He might even be expected to torture prisoners for information. All of this goes against the grain of any Honorable man. One must be willing to sacrifice his Honor for a greater cause. But the matter goes further still.

To take an enemy by stealth was dishonor enough, but in those ancient times, a major portion of a soldier's income came from stripping those fallen in battle. The dead, both friend and foe, were plundered of their armor, weapons and other valuables. In the course of scavenging, one might well find those who were still living. Perhaps they were mortally wounded and would soon die, perhaps they would live a few days or many weeks before dying; not the enemy only, but compatriots and friends. In those times, it was a certain death, and a Huntsman, experienced in these matters as he was, knew the signs. The wounded might actually survive only to be permanently maimed, paralyzed, blind or in lasting pain. Such a man would be discharged from service and become a "wrecche", a masterless man, having no source of income but beggary or theft. It was considered an act of mercy to dispatch such a one.

It is not difficult to comprehend the Huntsman's preoccupation with death when we understand the paradox surrounding the moral dilemma he faced. One might well plunder the dead enemy for one's own enrichment, one might even finish off a wounded, unarmed and helpless enemy. But what of a friend? We all know John 3:16 from the Gospel which tells us that Jesus laid down His life for us, but how many can quote First John 3:16 in the Epistles which reminds us that as Christ gave his life for us, we also should lay down our lives for our Brothers. And Jesus Himself said, "Greater love hath no man than this, that a man lay down his life for his friends." What then of his Honor; his very soul itself? Saint Paul declared that he would die for his fellow countrymen, Moses offered to take the sins of Israel. What then shall we do?

Those who were found yet alive but dying, if they were conscious or could be brought to consciousness, were comforted, examined to ascertain the degree of their wounds and treated. But should their condition prove terminal, what then? Should they be left in agony, to linger on? No, The Huntsman would hear their confession (which would later be relayed to a priest), then expertly open an artery, cut the jugular or deliver the coup de grace to the heart. Was this an act of cynical and brutal betrayal, or was it an act of sublime mercy? Wouldn't a man of Honor do as much for a dog? To relieve suffering in a swift death was an unqualified act of personal heroism, an act of infinite kindness and heartfelt sympathy. The Huntsman was generous to the point of placing his own soul in peril for the sake of his friend. The Huntsman shouldered the burden of that man's life and his eternal soul. He himself became a soul in peril having acted of his own accord. Certainly he could not asked the dying man if he wished to be put out of his misery. For the dying man to ask for death would have been complicity in his own death, nothing short of suicide, and in asking to die he would be guilty of inciting another to commit murder, thus doubling his sin.

Still it was a dubious moral situation at best, for both men knew only too well the custom. Certainly he could have asked to be allowed to live, but what then, should the Huntsman allow him to live, or should he finish the task and perhaps be guilty of murder instead of mercy? In any event, it was an ill deed for the sake of mercy. I'm reminded of what Friedrich Nietzsche said, "Dare to lead the life of the tragic man and you will be redeemed." Ah, but will he indeed? Pray God that you and I may never have to ask the question in earnest.

The Old Brothers never plundered those whom they dispatched. The helpless wounded who received the coup de grace were not to be pillaged by the one who delivered the stroke. It may be observed that wild ravens, upon discovering a trapped, wounded or dying animal, will swoop down and finish the pitiful animal, but then will retreat to a nearby tree and call other ravens to come and feast while he himself will not partake of his own kill because the prey was helpless. How much more will the War Raven feel pity than a soulless bird? How much more will he feel the guilt by having a soul and a conscience? To have acted otherwise would be to show more concern for one's own Honor and soul than for that of another, and any heroic action to save the wounded man may only increase or prolong his suffering unto death. I'm provoked to wonder how the physician can ask for compensation for his efforts when a patient dies? How has he earned a reward?

It is a bitter and tragic life to take on the mantle of a War Raven, but there is no other life worth living than the Life of Honor.

THE STORY OF THE BEAR MOTHER, I believe, perfectly explains the first initiation. A she-bear teaches her cubs to obey implicitly. When mother bear gives the signal, the cubs scamper up the nearest tree and stay there until called to come down. This is a valuable survival trait, it keeps the cubs safe when danger is near or when mom needs to go hunting alone. Sometimes the bear mother will test the kids by sending them up a tree and then going to hide and watch. Sometimes, after a long while, one or both of the cubs will decide on their own to venture down from the tree. That's when mom comes roaring out of the woods to give the disobedient little rascals a sound thrashing.

But the day finally comes when mom knows the boys are old enough to fend for themselves. That's the day she sends them up a tree and hightails it for parts unknown. One of two things will now happen, they will stay in that tree until they starve to death, or they will decide to DISOBEY mom. After several hours, perhaps even a couple of days, the bears usually decide to disrespect their mother's training and come down out of the tree. Thus the mother-bond is broken.

Among humans a similar thing happens. At some point, the child (especially a boy child) must decide to break the mother-bond. Most boys push the envelope from time to time throughout their childhood, but it's seldom a genuine bid for freedom, it's just "play". However, the day must surely come when the boy must make the real "break". Mom seldom holds still for this...you have to remember that this is her JOB: To test the boy's determination, self-reliance and competence. If he tries to make the break and she resists, he may cave-in and return to being a "good boy" tied to his mother's apron strings. Some men never seem to be able to escape mom's influence and control; he's always going to be her "good boy", no matter how old he is. Strangely enough, if he holds his ground and insists upon his freedom, at some point mom will capitulate. Oh she may test him again later on to see if he is sincere, but generally, once he has made the break, mom is content.

Our ancestors knew that age seven was optimum time to break the mother-bond. In former times a seven year old boy was usually fostered out to an uncle, a friend of the family, or someone skilled in the trade for which the boy was to be trained. Noble families sent their young sons to another household where they served as pages and learned social skills. At age fourteen it was expected that he would become a squire to a knight and at twenty one he would be knighted himself. A commoner would be fostered out as an apprentice, working his way up to journeyman and then to master of his craft by age twenty one. Our society has utterly corrupted this system over the past two hundred years. We now leave our children in the tender care of government-run institutions of learning which basically prepares them to make money and nothing else.

There is virtually nothing in Western Civilization that serves as valid, authoritative and effective rites of passage. Fortunately, the initiations of the Hunting Orders (being the most ancient and most securely linked to our genetic predisposition), serves as an almost perfect universal initiation system. You will notice that I said "almost"; not everyone is drawn to it. Some are, for whatever reason, absolutely repelled, terrified or simply disinterested. (I would like to see a study on this to learn if there is any correlation between initiates, those who reject the initiation and blood types A, B, and AB as opposed to type-O blood groups.)

In any event, the seven year old initiation seems to be ideally suited to gently and appropriately release the boy from maternal bondage. It happens at the right time, in the right way. Respect for one's mother is not shattered; in fact, I suspect the filial bond is probably strengthened in that the need to tear oneself away from mom is eliminated. The Anwalt has done it for the boy, and done it properly and "officially". There is no stress or resentment between mother and son in breaking the maternal ties.

Hunter/Gatherer societies had no calendars; they didn't need them. It was agrarian societies that needed exact readings of the time of the year in order to determine planting and harvesting. American Indian myths tell of Coyote, a Trickster figure, whose job it was to set things in order after everything was created. When it came to the stars, Coyote carefully placed the sun and moon, the pole star, the constellations of Orion and the Pleiades. Immediately, Coyote lost interest and just scattered all the rest of the stars and planets in random patterns. The stellar bodies described are useful to Hunters to know when autumn and spring are coming, to know the directions of the compass at night, to know the approximate seasons of the year and the time of day. The Hunter needed nothing else. Blame astrology on the farmers.

It struck me one day that perhaps the connection between Hunters and blacksmiths has something to do with the elements. Coal from the EARTH, FIRE from the forge, AIR from the bellows and WATER for quenching is what it takes to make copper, bronze or iron blades...and or course the blacksmith's HAMMER, the "changer" or "reconciler". Just a thought.

In further regard to astronomy and the like, I could wish to see the Roman names of the months done away with in favor of the old Folk names for the various months (moons), especially since the moon in October or November is called the Hunter's Moon. Roman names honor their gods, dead emperors and numbers; a patch-work of non-sense.

In the lore of those who dabble in the occult, there is a category of technology known as "psychotronic" devices. One such machine is called the Heironymous device; it does what it does with a total disre-gard for the known laws of physics. I once read about a man who was building an Heironymous device when he realized he had run out of copper wire. It suddenly occurred to him that since the device seemed to run on "psychic" energy anyway, copper wire ought to be superflu-ous, so he substituted plain cotton thread. He swore the machine worked perfectly. He then built yet another machine using ONLY the hand-drawn electronic schematic. This too worked just fine. I was reminded of those medieval alchemists and sorcerers who drew magical designs which they believed, properly applied, would grant them magi-cal powers. What is an electronic schematic if not just another "magical diagram"? This probably falls under the heading of "For every silly sci-entific theory, there is a perfectly valid supernatural explanation."

Remember my theory of the "Electricity Demon"? Who's to say that modern society isn't actually working hand-in-glove with the forces of Satan?

In Viking mythology, there is the story of the "Ship of Nails". It is a war ship made entirely from the nail parings of dead men. It was said that once the ship was completed, it would set sail, signaling the onset of Ragnarok, the catastrophic end of the world. The implication of the Ship of Nails is that the end of society (the end of the world as we know it) comes about by the cumulative neglect of simple, basic standards of personal grooming, hygiene, good manners, disciplined and orderly living. To die with "uncut nails" was to contribute to the eventual dissolution of the world. Thus, the practical application of the story was to warn people of the ultimate consequences of unprincipled living and that they should always keep their nails trimmed lest they should die unexpectedly and have something contributed to the Ship of Ragnarok. Only landless, masterless people had any excuse for going about dirty and unkempt, unprincipled and undisciplined.

When I was younger, I used to agonize over all the great things I would never get to do in life. Then one day, I received a revelation. The voice said, "You could have done much, but there is not room for everyone to do all they want, it would crowd out others and deprive them of opportunities. It doesn't matter that you have no talent (and you do have talent). All that matters is that someone, somewhere did it, that someone experienced it. It is enough that it happened at all. Because it was done by someone, it was done by you. It is enough that you wished it so, for you shall know even as you are known; fully, absolutely, perfectly and constantly forever. Knowing this, it is your duty to go right on being human, coping with family difficulties, making a living, catching colds, paying bills, growing old and dying with Honor. All this is every bit as important as creating great art, inventing flying machines or curing cancer."

Men are not "driven" by ambition, they are held back by ambition. It is a burden, a stumbling-block, a detour, a constraint, a hostage situation, if you will. They are deceived and diverted. Ambition is a millstone around men's necks, forcing them to devote endless hours of time, attention, energy and resources toward an ever-receding goal. Ambition is an ugly and shameful perversion growing out of a man's secret fears and insecurities. It drives him to seek to be exalted above his peers, to seek power over his peers, and the worst of it is that our society condones, encourages and idolizes power and ambition.

A drowning man isn't rational, you can't reason with him. The drowning man cannot think for himself, nor should he be allowed to under the guise of "freedom of expression". A potential rescuer must do whatever it takes to save the drowning man's life, no matter how the drowning man may struggle and fail or refuse to cooperate. If the rescuer doesn't take control, the drowning man will surely drown and may pull the inept rescuer down with him. But what choice do we have? The man who could be a rescuer but only stands on the beach and yells instructions to the drowning man is worse than useless. To simply stand silently and watch makes him a stupid spectator. Such a one may be concerned for the drowning man's freewill, freedom of self-determination and the right to his own befuddled attitudes and actions, but the drowning man will still drown. Those who stand by and watch are moral cowards, irresponsible, uncaring, incompetent and disgusting. A rescuer must do what he must do to save the man; knock him out if need be, certainly he must exercise absolute control over the man until he gets him to shore. Perhaps the man will prove to be a fool and charge his rescuer with overzealous and unasked-for intervention, perhaps he will even try to sue him in court for failing to mind his own business or for using excessive force, but would you rather be sued for negligent homicide or failure to render aid in standing quietly by while someone died? Remember, in this court, God will be the Judge.

I have only recently learned that two of the more common punishments decreed against early Christians who refused to recant their Faith, was to have one eye put out or to have the muscles of one leg cut. These mutilations would come to be seen as badges of authority and distinction marking those who were absolutely loyal to the Faith and therefore absolutely trustworthy; men of principle and Honor. Perhaps our tradition of the one-eyed man, the lame man and the hanged man stems from this. It is certain that the one-eyed lame man as a man of character goes far back into antiquity and mythology. Alexander the Great was called "Son of the one-eyed man", referring to his father, Phillip of Macedon, who was both one-eyed and walked with a severe limp.

The Truth will make you free, it will also condemn the guilty in a court of law. The Truth can ennoble or shame. For every man set free by the Truth, a thousand are condemned. There are many "truths" which do not deserve to be made public. Just because it is true doesn't make it Truth. We must always ask: Who is to profit from so-called "truth"?

Have our lives been enriched by knowing Thomas Jefferson was a fornicator? Has the Hemings family been elevated to honor by the publication of their ancestor's debauchery? What child is now happier or a better person for knowing this? Who is uplifted to learn George Washington had wooden dentures or that U.S. Grant was a drunk? It only makes the small man feel large and the corrupt self-justified. And even this is a fiction, a comforting lie for the wicked. As Saint Paul said, "Evil should not even be named among you." The very fact that we openly discuss abortion and portray all manner of evil in our films and television programming, music and literature is an evil itself. To discuss it "clinically" only serves to sanitize it for "polite society". If such topics were treated as shameful, they would become shameful; they would cease to be imitated and practiced. Indeed, most people would never imagine such things had they not been so carefully instructed about them by the media and the "social engineers".

Speaking of "evil", let's talk about money. What's money got to do with Honor? Everything! Money is, perhaps, the greatest stumbling block we face. Money was invented as a MEDIUM of exchange, not the REASON for exchange. Money was never meant to be the "motive" for business. In ancient times, men conducted trade for mutual benefit...not to get the other guy's money. Trade was a wholesome and honorable exchange of goods and services. It was also the "polite thing to do". It was mutual generosity.

(You may find it difficult to grasp the real message here. We are deeply immersed in the "profit motive" and often have a hard time making the radical "mind-shift" back to the original concept of trade. It may even require a "break through" on your part that no written explanation can provide.)

It is natural for most of us to want to give gifts to those we like. This often results in their returning the favor at some point in the future. We want to "enrich" them; it's a token of our esteem. And having them graciously accept our gift "enriches" us.

But suppose they insist on paying us for the gift. Most people, even today, will be insulted by someone who insists on paying cash for a gift offered out of simple kindness and friendship. If pressed to accept money, they might say things like, "What do you think I am? I'm not looking for a hand-out! What am I, a doorman, that you try to give me a tip or a pay-off?" We instinctively understand that those who insist on paying for a gift or kindness actually wish to avoid any personal indebtedness to you. They want to be free of owing you courtesy in return; they can do this by getting you to accept cash instead. By paying for what he receives he effectively "washes his hands" of any social obligation to you. To accept cash payment or something in direct trade is to acknowledge the social obligation as paid in full. To accept payment for a courtesy, gift or service is to place yourself in an inferior social position. You have no further claim on that man's friendship; he has refused you his friendship by paying for your gesture of friendship.

The true "currency" of manhood in a healthy society is Honor. Today we think a good credit rating establishes our "honor". A bad credit rating may establish our lack of honor, but a good credit rating says nothing about the presence of Honor. In past times a man relied on his Honor to get along in life. Today we rely on being cash-flush. Money and Honor; the more you value one, the less you will value the other. It is absolutely unavoidable.

There was a time when the only true measure of a man was his Honor. Today we are not asked to pledge our word, we are asked to put down a deposit, a cash bond, earnest money. If we go to court and are proven guilty we don't much care about our Honor being impuned, we're concerned about how much money we must pay in fines and court costs. Indeed, our punishment is set in dollars instead of the loss of Honor.

We live in a culture where a man's power is external to himself. This power is in the form of cash. Money has become the measure of the man. But money is very arbitrary, it doesn't care who it serves. Even a child with money can exercise power…as we have all seen! But only so long as that child has money! Any fool or madman with money has power. Crude and abusive people with money are treated like kings for the sake of their ready cash. We "respect" those with money. When money is the measure of our power, our deep-seated insecurities are perpetuated because we know our power is not of ourselves. Free yourself from the power of money and you can smell the powerlessness of the wealthy.

When our Nation was founded, courtesy, Honor and goodwill was still currency. A man could ride from one end of the Colonies to the other with little or no money in his pocket. He could rely on the courtesy, Honor and consideration of people along the way to provide him with a night's lodging, care for his horse, a hot meal and directions to his destination. All that was expected in return was good company and gratitude. His hosts would have been profoundly insulted had he insisted upon paying for what he received. They knew that the time would come when they themselves would need the same assistance and that they would receive it by virtue of the fact that they had granted it to others. This was considered the natural order of things. Both the guest and the host believed in doing good for others. They were men of Honor.

Careful examination of the Law of Moses and the Gospel of Christ shows us that all of the teachings of the Prophets and the Apostles was based firmly on the rules of etiquette, courtesy, kindness and generosity. Even worship of God Himself was founded on rules of hospitality and courtesy.

Why have we come to place our confidence in money? Money is not a safer, surer commodity. "A fool and his money are soon parted." One's life savings can vanish with one bad investment, inflation, economic collapse, theft, or a lavish lifestyle.

We've all paid "good money" for worthless merchandise or services, so why do we think money is somehow "foolproof"? There are many things money can't get for you...at any price! You can't "buy" happiness, friends or love. But Honor can secure all of these things for you.

Why are our initiations sometimes allowed within sight of ruined buildings or even within the confines of a ruined building? I believe it is because they stand as a monument to the victory of the natural order of God's Creation over the presumptions and false realities of human society imposed upon nature.

How did Cain make a living? The ground had already been cursed because of Adam, now the already diminished strength of the earth was forbidden to yield at all to cultivation by Cain. I suggest that Cain may have become a thief and a forager. Scripture says "A fugitive and vagabond". One who gathers wild plants that grow of themselves for his food can't settle in one place, but must keep moving in an endless search for edible wild plants. To supplement his food supply, he must have taken up stealing from those who could farm…which explains why those who found him would want to kill him. The mark which God put on Cain was a warning and an object of great fear; people somehow knew they couldn't take revenge on Cain's theft without dire consequences…seven times worse! It is reasonable to assume that Cain, already an unrepentant murderer, wouldn't hesitate to turn this to his advantage and set himself up as a local "warlord". How else could one who couldn't farm and didn't hunt (nobody ate meat in his generation) afford to build a "city"; a permanent dwelling place? From his fortified position, he could dominate the surrounding area and demand "taxes" from the local farmers who could raise food for him. In effect, Cain and his family became the first hereditary de facto "kings", who spent all their time developing political power and TECHNOLOGY.

The Raven's Bread obviously contains acorns, but how is it made? Acorns must be ground into meal then leached with water until all the tannic acid is washed out. This is accomplished when the drained water ceases to have a "milky" appearance. Taste the acorn meal, if it still has a bitter taste, leach it still more until the bitterness is washed away. Acorn meal can be added to many foods, but for our purposes it is made into bread. It is often mixed with wheat flour. In fact, even a small amount of acorn meal is adequate as a "token" to qualify it as Acorn Bread.

"Compromise" used to be a dirty word in our society; it means to transgress one's principles. A compromise is a situation in which no one is well served. Truly, a compromise promises that the wolves will have mutton for dinner but no sheep will be eaten.

Stories of your own youthful mistakes are better than platitudes. They absolve the boy of stupidity because you were stupid, but they obligate him to learn from his mistakes because you did.

You may find an old man foolish, but never call him a fool. You may doubt his wisdom, but you must never doubt his experience. An old man may appear ridiculous, but never ridicule him. You may ignore his advice, but never ignore the old man himself. You may doubt his word, but never dispute it. You may not respect the old man, but never be discourteous to him. Never so much as wink at a friend in the old man's presence. You may be thought entertaining, you may even gain preeminence among your peers, but you will never be thought wise or worthy of leadership...and someday another young man will smile and wink at a friend in your presence.

He will never rise to true authority who has no respect for authority.
He that wishes to do good hires the poor. He that wished to appear good scatters coins among the rabble.

Charity is reserved for the elderly and infirm. The promise of a gift corrupts the shiftless.

Teach the indolent and wayward to work. Those who feed the lazy seek to enslave them.

Throw bread to a dog and he will come to sleep on your doorstep.

Evil men seek to buy the support of the people with gifts.

The poor accept bribery with envy and resentment. The rabble will always turn on their masters in the end.

Those who live in darkness all their lives think the light is evil because it hurts their eyes.

Those who don't want their business known, miss a lot of business.

Teach a daughter modesty within the family and she won't be so quick to get naked with those outside the family.

To gain a man's goodwill, don't loan him money, borrow money from him and pay it back promptly.

Teach the virtues and the values will follow. Teach the values and the virtues will follow.

ARCHETYPE: The original pattern or model from which all things of a like nature are derived. A prototype. An inherited idea or mode of thought that is derived from the cumulative experience of the race and is present in the unconscious of the individual. An instinct. An inborn comprehension of an idea or a mode of thought or behavior, such as an infant's instinctive fear of falling.

SYMBOL: An act, sound or object having cultural significance and the capacity to excite or objectify a response. An object or action that represents an unconscious association. Something that stands for or suggests something else by reason of association, relationship, convention or coincidental resemblance. A visible sign of something invisible… "The lion is a symbol of courage."

SYMBOLISM: Expressing the invisible or intangible by means of visible or sensory representations.

ARCHETYPAL SYMBOLISM: A "language" which evokes an active response through unconscious associations.

Initiations of the Hunting Orders are instruction by means of Archetypal language. That's the only language the right hemisphere of the brain understands. One must speak this language as an authority figure (an Elder, Father of the Tribe, Master of the Hunt) or speak as his authorized agent.

If you speak to me in French, you will think me a fool and I will learn nothing, I'm not French! I can't respond to any instruction in French. If you give me information, a command, permission to act, I cannot benefit by that instruction. If you speak to me in English but have no authority, I may doubt or reject your instruction. Should I choose to act on your instruction, I may find it useless, or I may find myself in a good deal of trouble for having followed the directives of someone with no authority to issue directives.

Books are of limited value. They serve only as road signs to point you to someplace where you can get proper instruction. I have both heard and read the Presidential Oath of Office, it hasn't made me President of the United States of America. Reciting it aloud won't make me President. Not even having a Supreme Court Justice administer the oath to me will make me President. I must first be elected, then sworn in. Even so, while I may hold the Office, I may still prove incompetent and unworthy of the Presidency. I need initiation.

When we know something in a deep, meaningful way, or when we know something seemingly beyond our natural senses, we might say, "I feel it in my bones." This is a profound expression. The very word "symbol" means "A piece of the bone" (a piece representing the whole). The bones are the foundational structure of a person, symbolic of the deepest inner self. Conventional language doesn't speak to the inner man. We must "speak the Bones" in order to speak TO the bones.

An obvious question: How can a trip to the woods for some archaic hunting ritual make a man out of a boy; make him competent, reliable, resourceful, insightful, considerate of his fellow human beings…in short, all the things we think a man should be?

Let's change the question a little. How does a hawk teach its young to fly? Certainly not by nagging, not by verbal instruction, not by long formal training in aerodynamics with charts, math problems and flight simulators. No, the adult hawk first gives the young permission to leave the nest, then coaxes them to leap off the cliff. Instinct kicks in and they soar up into the sky.

All babies are born knowing how to nurse; the pupils of their eyes contract automatically in bright light. The first is instinct, the second is reflex. All they need to perform these acts is the right opportunity or stimulus. It happens without instruction. Many children, with no formal training, teach themselves to play a musical instrument or to draw, but it can't happen unless they have the materials and opportunity. Most of what happens in the initiation process is about authorization and permission. Permission to get on with life.

For the most part, western culture fails or refuses to give permission to move on to maturity. And in ten thousand ways discourages or diverts that process.

◆   ◆   ◆

Many a truth has lost its way traversing the labyrinths of time and history, never again to grace the lives and thoughts of men. I have pledged myself that this shall not be so with the Wisdom of the Hunt. Success doesn't depend upon me, but upon you. Much of what I've said in these pages will seem foreign and enigmatic. Some of it will seem like foolishness and perhaps it is; after all, I'm all too human myself. I have not told one tenth of what I would like to. I have previously written another manuscript on this Tradition (from a different perspective) and I have several POUNDS of notes collected up over the past thirty years and more. There are a good many topics which I have not even hinted at. What I have discussed has been merely hints. But I have certainly provided you with the basics; the means to begin, and you have the opportunity to learn more than I ever have.

I promised the Brothers before I began this present work, to keep it short and instructional; to keep it as closely tied to the initiation process as possible. Should this book find its mark and if there is further demand, God willing, I will continue the Wisdom of the Hunt in a second volume, or perhaps an ongoing news letter…or perhaps, not at all!

As with all things pertaining to the Tradition of the Hunt, there are four things and a fifth. And so it is with this book. The fifth and final part (not counting the appendix of illustrations, endorsement/disclaimer by the Brotherhood, and the list of recommended reading) is a collection of poems, insights and inspirations which I have penned over the years. For some readers, this will say more than many volumes. I thank you for your time and attention.

Songs of the Hunt

GOD'S MAN

On the High Path the Sun comes early—A sweet peace lies upon the land—And in the valley below, the forest still sleeps in deep, cool shadow—The Shining Wheel climbs higher and pours out its Life on the peaks—And they shine—They turn pink and then gold as the warming rays glide down the path toward the mists below—Then the mountain itself awakens and lives—And a vibration begins in the roots of this tower of earth and stone—A deep, gentle pitch, like the tone of a cello, a note held long and soft, no longer heard, but only felt—An early wanderer sings and strikes mellow chords on an ancient and weathered lute—Oaks and willows listen and nod their approval in the sweet morning breeze—Spring is still new—The Sun is welcome as it touches hair and cheek—The breeze brings promise of yet cool spring rains—The grass is short and green—Wild flowers bright and new—It is the spring of a year unnamed and without number—Only a year among years, a time out of time, a place out of time, ancient but not old—A time of twilight although it is dawn—The man is young but weighed down with the Ages—The trees about him are hardly more than saplings, but the forest stands silent in its primordial wisdom—Children already dance and play in the meadow—Wild flowers entwined in sun bleached curls—The wanderer watches, smiles and remembers—The dust of many lands cover his boots and the laughter of other children have filled his ears—And he must move on for there are yet other lands—He sees ahead an outcropping of stone—A couch of granite and an Oak for shade to enjoy his breakfast of cheese and crusty bread—A deep, clear pool ripples and sparkles in the Sunlight

142

before him—From among the pebbles at his feet he chooses a stone—Flat, round and tarnished—tiny lines still remain along one edge—"IN GOD WE TRUST"—If the wanderer had read, he would have agreed—It skipped happily across the Sun dappled water.

—Dolph 1966

CONSIDER THE LILIES

No one took notice as the Sun rose today
None studied its path as it went on its way
None but the sea birds traversing the sky
And not even they mark the seasons gone by

Away in the distance the pulsing sea can be heard. But here only the trees stand to listen. Winter has at last retreated up the mountain again, but still a few snowy fingers stretch down the newly greened slopes and onto the fresh alpine meadow, a favorite gathering place for the smaller animals. All manner of furry, skittering creatures congregate to nibble sweet clover buds and tender shoots. Bright butterflies sail silently about, black and gold banded bees carefully drain the minute drops of nectar from a bright array of wild flowers, and at the same time, unknowingly pollinate the young blossoms, thereby insuring another year's supply of sweetness. And so life glides on as before, as indeed it should, balanced and unmolested. The lee has grown and bloomed untrampled for many seasons. Birds sing and teach their young to fly year after year without interruption. So many generations have come and gone that even the most shy animals have grown bold and adventuresome again. At times the lynx or coyote happens upon the little community, but then it is only to take their rightful share of the sick and old. All has been provided, all needs have been met. Even the curiosity of the Swaggering Crow can be aroused and appeased as he slips down to examine a bright sparkle at the edge of the meadow,

Pleased to find something to while away the time, he lands directly before it and introduces himself in raucous tones of conceit. Receiving no answer, he cocks his head first to the left and then to the right, each black eye surveying in turn the shining nugget. Thinking to carry it away, he pecks once, twice and again, but it stands fast and refuses to be liberated as spoils. No matter, none other can take it either, and he can return again and again. Many happy moments of contemplation and companionship lie ahead for the Raven and the tilted, half-buried skull with the gold tooth. The over-grown crow will speak of far places and his own brave deeds. Old skull will listen politely and smile grimly at the black bird's simple vanities, for he himself was once a master of vanities. But now his sockets are empty and shattered. Always they were blind, and now they are sightless. A tawny little field mouse abides in the left cavity, a single lily thrives in the other. So at last, even man has found a permanent, useful place in Nature's scheme. He doesn't complain of his fate, nor plot against the mouse, nor begrudge him his window box of lilies. Nor will he think to rebuke the brash and brazen little braggart of a crow for his ceaseless rhetoric. For in the words of Omar, "Their mouths at last are stopped with dust." The Eagle again is lord of the skies.

—Dolph 1966

THE LEPER'S BELL

Autumn rains, cold and lonely, tiny crystal globes descending from skies of old pewter, clicking faintly upon crisp leaves of red and gold, wind rustling dry grass and brown sheaves of corn stalks, the smell of hickory from antique chimney pots, innocent pumpkins, soon to be endowed with impish grins and glowing eyes that see goblins and bats flitting across the face of an orange moon, frost, like diamond dust, reflecting chips of light from the warm, early morning sun, the very air frozen and brittle, the call of a bird, sharp and clear, the feel of woolen coats and creaking leather boots, an air of expectancy, even though all of nature seems suspended, then a wisp of cloud, blowing high, driven steadily on by a wind that rattles the very stones of the iron gray mountain, bringing crystals of snow, the soul of the rain drop, shaped by the hands of angels to reveal its form, a time when the dull, unseeing and unbelieving sigh and grumble of hardships and discomforts, and seek shelter from the works of God, but also a time when the living lift up their eyes and see adventure in every trembling pine needle, the cry of the Valkyries comes riding on the shoulders of a wild north wind, and the heart sings, a time to take up the palmer's staff and go in search of that which has not yet been seen or done, those who are short of thought and love turn away from the music of autumn for they hear only the tinkling of the leper's bell, but the living hear the chimes of Christmas.

—Dolph October 1965

TWENTIETH CENTURY QUEST

Rabble and babble ptomaine propane profane
A stab in the back little hope lotta pain
Prelate premonition agate and scot
Words I can't use lie here and rot
Away to the east up north and then down
When I open my mouth they think I'm a clown
Fig Newton grandma Moses book of the dead
Classics I've seen comics I've read
The prophet the moppet Shirley temple the cool
A lion is dangerous so is a fool
Blunder asunder rockets and pox
Scarlet red ribbons and dirty sweat socks
Words by the dozens like so many cousins

They come and they go they ebb and they flow
Off to the mountain to bathe in a fountain
Whittle and fiddle awake and a doze
If you don't like my poetry don't turn up your nose
Glasses and grasses euthanasia and all
Suspended animation crustaceans do crawl
Ruminate consummate gelatin flask
Promotion commotion a Halloween mask
Lenin in linen exclusive abusive
Off they go somewhere I know
Flying about like winter snow
Cossack cassock are they the same
As Shakespeare would say what's in a name
Squirrel pearl Katmandu
Voltaire the mighty epileptic Zulu
Incest insect sister cistern
Lute loot blessed her blister
Opium opiate a blackberry cobbler
Let's say a prayer for the Thanksgiving gobbler
Mitgard retard forklift adrift
Critical political hydromantic shift
Box cars nova stars cellophane wrapper
Rochambeau all aglow a 1920 flapper
Guillotine Benzedrine prism prison
Acme acne nuclear fission
Listen and christen a pneumatic drill
Don't try to stop me til I've written my fill
Plasma plastic a transparent bodice
Twentieth century please tell me...Quo Vadis?

—Dolph November 1966

STORM RAVEN

The wind rushes through the forest sweeping dry leaves and pine needles before it, exposing the damp brown earth to the open sky. The sun is high above, twinkling through the leaves and struggling branches, touching the forest floor here and there with searching fingers of gold. Slender beams seeking a place to hold fast as the ragged clouds overwhelm the face of the sun-wheel leaving it a great luminous white pearl, and still it fades and the shadows die with it. The land seems to draw a cloak of shade over its body and the trees cry out and the stones murmur and grow cold. A great dead Oak stands alone—an outcast, twisted and decaying like a barrow marker of some long dead king…and it howls in anxiety. The clouds rumble and threaten the end of all things. The mountains gather themselves up and reach out to defend the land below. The falcon descends from the high cliffs, for the face of the mountain is wet and dripping. So even the birds of prey must escape the wrath to come. The old gnarled Oak offers protection from the dark mists threading among the weathered boles. The falcon ruffles his feathers and positions his black talons securely on the dusky bark. Lightning flashes in the north like a twisting trident, cords of yellow and white fire violently illuminating the cold hard mountains and momentarily lighting the path for a whirlwind of dust and leaves—a frenzied wraith escaped from a moldering tomb and flogging the land in madness. A cry, as of some demented soul, rose from the throat of the falcon, it's jaundiced eyes agleam. The black curved beak flicked quickly away from the fading glow in the north. The piercing, emotionless gaze fell on a dark figure. Did the lightning reveal him to the attention of the assassin of rodents, or did the dark groping mind somehow know that he would appear at that moment? And I saw him there, as in a dream, as perhaps it was, a tall gaunt figure in a heavy gray mantle, a wide brimmed hat with a low spherical crown hid his features. He leaned heavily upon an old worn staff as the wind pelted his back impotently with dry, brittle leaves. And the tatters of his shadowed cloak flapped and fluttered before him, and for a moment exposed a sword slung at his side, the chape of which was curiously fashioned like a serpent's tail, the throat a viper's head and venomous jaws, the sheath bound in the skin of a reptile. The toes of his boots were pointed and turned up. His left hand clutched at his cloak and drew it up around his throat. And upon that ancient and calloused hand he bore the phoenix ring. That dread talisman, its symbols bearing no magic or power of their own save the ability to inspire good or evil in the heart of the wearer according to the inclination of his soul. Wrought of silver, that one precious metal which can glow like the sun or tarnish black as night. At once the symbol of wealth and power or virtue and greatness—thirty shekels or a silver chalice—never was there another, never will another be.

What is this madness and this man? I will not tell thee. And who am I? I am the Raven, neither this nor that, only the soul in peril that flies before the storm seeking refuge among the towers of Theopolis. And the ring?…it is as I have said.

—Dolph 1966

THE FOUR WINDS OF HEAVEN

The wanderer knows the land from Tenochtitlan to Samarkand and Ages past from first to last and times untold to him unfold.

This is the time, the goal of time, it has reached its destination and now it rests. The lion and the unicorn sleep in peace. The eagle and the bear drowse eternally and the dragon has devoured itself in a fit of madness—and the Sun is soon to rise. Already the waxwing stirs from slumber and begins its chatter as the nighthawk folds its wings in sleep. The constellations fade one by one and Venus arises pointing the way for a greater star. Only the brighter stellar fires remain, infinitely distant jewels adorning the fingers of angels. Sweeping above broken clouds, the moon glides to rest full and orange, into a dark and whispering sea. The sheep will awaken on this day and have no fear of the rampant lion. And this is the beginning of the day—not another day, just the day—for yesterday is a ghost and tomorrow only a promise. In the night man fears his enemy and death, but with morning hope is restored. The peasant in his stone cottage lies sleeping and dreams of fertile meadows and orchards mellow and heavy. Only the Raven croaks and winks as he ponders the thoughts of dying men and takes note of the passing seasons—so swiftly the years of men—the vulture is extinct for the provender of the battlefield is no more.

And none save one remains to remember and this wanderer must earn
his meat and mead
By singing the legends of heroes and deeds dead and forgotten
A thousand years and more
Then moves on at dusk and entreats at another door
His boots in the dust his eyes on the sky
He smiles at the birds for they know not they can fly
Then he weeps and he laughs at the follies of men
And takes up his lute and begins all again
The histories and ages
Of poets and sages
And he dreams of a girl with golden red hair
That curls and twists like a pillar of smoke
And velvet puff sleeves that billow and float
As she rides out early in the morning breeze
And of old bottled wine
And grapes yet on the vine
Hot buttered rum
And a toasted warm bun
Chestnuts aplenty
And brown ale for a penny

And stags there are running in forest and mark
And pine cones to gather when out on a lark
The woodlands go marching away to the east
And somewhere beyond there
Waits his holiday feast
The river and poplar are his in the spring
To sit and ponder and sometimes sing
But a cottage and lamp he seeks in the fall
When it's cold and damp he sings best of all
For then he remembers the wisdom he holds
The secrets of men that cannot be told
And the burden of knowledge is terribly great
So he sings in a riddle the whisperings of fate
Always the towers of Theopolis he sees
Beyond the stone mountain beyond the green trees
He travels by day and rests then at night
The towers glow pink in the sun's fading light
By morning they're silver and farther away still
Across one more river over one more hill
And yet he knows not his pilgrimage would halt
If only he learned that he was at fault
The four winds of Heaven blow cold in the fall
And he's pushed along with them, the four of them, all.

—Dolph 1966

PLIGHT OF THE DREAMER

Had I no enemies to wish I'd die
I'd dream on things of days gone by

Of castles white on mountains high
A splendid dream for the romantic mind
Yet I dare not sleep and I know not why
I want to stay though I know I'll die
Sword in hand and battle cry
To stand in Honor—they're drawing nigh
One long moment more and my soul shall fly
Dream castles are real, reality a lie
Of this I dreamed and so must die

—Dolph 1964

A DESERT DREAM

I dreamed of standing in the midst of a great barren desert at the edge
of a long canal reaching from horizon to horizon. The canal was
blocked by tall iron floodgates set between rugged shoulders of stone.
They were black and scaled, as if blasted by some intense heat. Threads
of water leaked in tiny rivulets from its weakened seams. I climbed
down the face of the cliff and beat my fists against the floodgates with
violence and determination. The black scales of iron oxide rattled
down like dry leaves from the reverberating doors. The leaks increased.
I climbed up the opposite wall and stopped about half way up to turn
and watch as the bound and riveted doors creaked and slowly opened.
Tons of cool blue water rushed through. As I watched in amazement, I
asked, "What was that?", and a voice said, "That was the Church." And
I turned and climbed on upward.

—Dolph 1966

WEDNESDAY'S CHILD

It was a most unusual place to find a scholar, to say the least, but that's where I found him, an Old Man pondering wisdom in the Wilderness. I had set out earlier than usual that day and had covered a good distance when I spied a heavy-racked stag grazing at the edge of a woodland. I had no need of food for the hunting had been plentiful and my rucksack was just as heavy as I cared to carry. Yet, being a hunter, it was not in me to let the beast go entirely. So I decided to afford myself a small diversion and stalk the animal for amusement. I trailed the stag until the Sun was high and finally found myself within stone's throw of the beast, feeling elated at my prowess as a Huntsman, for not once had the wary stag sensed my presence. Resolving to teach him a lesson for his carelessness, I pelted him with a handful of gravel and bellowed like a ravenous bear. Away he bounded, startled out of his wits. I laughed aloud as he disappeared into the glen. How I had frightened the poor creature. By now the morning was spent, so hoisting my gear, I trudged on, following the same path the stag had taken in flight. I had not gone half a league till it brought me upon a clearing which sloped gently to the edge of a shear granite cliff. There, sitting on a stone in the shade of a gnarled oak, was the Old Man. He gazed longingly across the valley toward the mountains of the West. Without turning, he called to me. "You've tarried long, come and sit." I was amazed, for I had not made a sound as I approached the clearing, and he surely had not seen me.

As I drew near, I saw he was seated upon an ancient and weathered stone covered with runes and pictures. At his feet lay a tumble of books, scrolls, sheaves of paper and charts. Eyeing all of this and seeing no threat in it, I laid aside my pack and sat cross-legged on the ground beside him. "How did you know I was there?" I asked. "Who are you Old Man, what do you here among the mountains and forest?"

"You wish to know much, young one." He replied, still not setting eyes on me, "But I perceive it is only the idle curiosity of the moment.

Still you must be told". He sighed. "My name is Kronos", he said. "It is not a name I took from the Greeks, it is a name they took from me. I knew you were there because I have been waiting for you. The stag led you directly here and told me you were near."

"You play old men's games with me, Grandfather", I growled. "No one speaks with the beasts of the wood. Now state your business and I will be gone. I have far to go and I'm in a hurry."

"Be not impatient, little Raven. Yes, you see I know your name. Sit still and I will explain all."

Now more curious than ever, I sat quietly while the Old One collected his thoughts. "It is late", he said, "We have been apart too long and must begin immediately." "What do you mean, Old Man?" "I have never set eyes on you till this moment, and what common ground can there be for an alliance between us, or that we should desire the companionship of one another?"

"To us", he said, "it has been given, by God Himself, to fulfill a commission. To me, it is to learn. I shall seek knowledge among all whom you meet. To learn, one must observe closely, but to scrutinize the world too closely is to lose the joy of it. Therein lies your task; God has given you to go and see and impart the evidence to me. I may not touch the world, but you must. I shall unravel the mysteries which you find."

"What, am I only your slave, then?" I roared. "Am I to simply go hither and yon at your bidding? Never, you old fool. I have things of my own to do!"

"Nevertheless, you shall do it." He nodded.

"Now you threaten me!" I growled. And drawing my dagger, I pinioned a sheaf of papers to the ground in protest. With bared teeth I mocked him. "Is this the weapon with which you will bind me to your will…a few scraps of paper? Useless knowledge? Useless theories? I think not!" I growled in a low guttural whisper.

"You have not heard me out, Raven", he replied, "when you have, you will understand."

"I will understand nothing", I shouted. "Your babbling is senseless and only confuses me. I will have no part of it, and I will not be your servant."

At this he took up a twig and began sketching in the sand at his feet. "Listen a bit further," he said, "then decide. Do you know who you are?' He asked. Then, before I could think to answer, he continued, "No, you do not. You know not who you are, nor where you come from, nor whither you are bound…is it not so? You say you are in a hurry, but where are you going? Indeed, do you know now where you are? You are just a little wild bird wandering here and there, but soon you must become flesh. Oh, I see you are startled. Don't be dismayed. It is a hard thing to explain or understand, but we must both enter the flesh as one; in the same form. We shall travel together while we each seek our own direction. Ultimately we shall be reconciled to each other and the task at hand. Then will be the end of that task. Otherwise we can never climb the mountains of the west and stand before God."

"I know that as a man, one must serve God", I said, "But what is the nature of this service?" I asked.

"I know not", the Old Man answered, "But we shall learn through each other. We shall gain that which is required of us to perform that service."

Seeing that this was commanded of God and must not be resisted, I had no choice but to follow the Old Man as he arose, and to help him along the path downward toward the valley below, and toward the foot of the mountain which lay in the hazy distance before us.

"Who will he be?" I asked. "Will he be a great man among his people?"

"That I know not", the Old Man sighed. "All I know now is his name. He is of the clan of The Wolf."

"The connotation gives me hope", I responded, "I will rest my confidence on this name, it pleases me well."

"I'm sure it does." The Old One chuckled.

"And what of his given name?" I asked further.

"It gives no real clue", he said, "It is the name of a saint, but a doubting saint. Besides, it is the diminutive of that name, which suggests he could only be a very small and profane saint at best."

"Well enough", I said, "We shall make him a man and he shall have a chance—and a chance is all anyone can ask."

—Dolph 1966

THE DREAMING DEMON

It is dusk, the last month of the year, and from my window I see the skeletons of Oak trees. They stand black against a gray and drizzling sky. Crooked, angular fingers, upturned claws, straining to grasp the hand of spring. The black ones stand patiently, quivering and sighing. The awareness of another Age, another world, reaches me, searching me out, drawing me. And in the night they point to the constellation Orion as it courses the heavens and they whisper, "Look there." These carven acorns and Oaken leaves become dragons and unicorns about a crumbling tower with dead vines creeping in at the portals. A single spark of light glows from the ramparts, and there the Raven croaks and blinks and scratches the dry, dusty stones and laughs. The dark trunk is a doorway between worlds, and through it I gaze upon knights and bishops, sages and Saracens, poets and lute players. They stand and gaze back at me expressionless. They know me and our minds are in agreement without speaking. They have been expecting me. Many a secret the Oak whispers to me—of nova-like suns in deep black skies where infinity folds back upon itself, filled with celestial fires. A myriad of jewels, glowing rubies, emeralds, amethysts and pearls. And human figures, frozen like the ink in a Beardsley drawing. Their hair and limbs flow and drift, but never move. I see the coming of the Golden Horde, but the people listen not. I laugh from my vantage point, for I see the messenger child bearing news of the approaching plague. The people are doomed but do not listen. The Prophet exhorted them saying, "Let us pray." And they turned to their brothers and said, "Give heed to the Profit, let us prey." I saw them tease and entice a dreaming demon. One day they shall be found within his grasp, their bodies pierced and bleeding. And the ancient tree dwelt on other things and murmured the lamentations of the wanderer. The sonnets of old, the minstrel on the road, the words of the poet—the wisest of fools, and the philosopher—the most foolish of the wise. I peer through the lattice of twigs and branches to infinity great, and then at the dust of the earth to infinity small, and I see that they are nearer to each other than I am to either. In the beginning is the end. Is not the end of the circle also the starting? And somewhere the atom of the atom meets the galaxy of the galaxy and they join and are one. Cosmos without end. That which was is and shall be. The only inconsistent factor in a consistent and perfect universe is the spirit in rebellion. But then I realized that even man is but the length of a thought from the mind of God. And still the demon is dreaming…but he isn't sleeping.

—Dolph 1966

MYTH AND MEMORY

Here am I in a world I never made, a cause I never died for, a pilgrim in barbary. So I sit and gaze at the open flames, and the Raven takes flight on wings of black fire. Every time and place is mine. Like the wandering Jew of legend, I must go and search all things. I glide between heaven and earth as the Ages flash and fade before me. The moon rolls in an arc above me and looks on in astonishment. I see the bright colors of the winds, I feel them whipping about me and see them brushing and grooming the fields and trees. I descend to find myself standing in a ruined Norman castle, pondering a coat of arms; brown lions and unicorns, carved on an Oaken plaque, now weathered and filled with worm holes. Then, blown by the wind, I am away, across the face of time, sitting before a large open fireplace in a mountain cabin. I hear the slow rhythmic ticking of a wall clock. I turn in my chair to look out at the evening rain as it drips from the pine trees near the front walk. From somewhere the aroma finds me; the warm, almost forgotten smell of freshly parched peanuts. And then I'm lifted away from this peace and solitude. Now I'm standing guard in a watch tower overlooking the Russian steppe. Wrapped in furs against the brittle winter dawn, my fingers numbly grip an iron shod spear. My eyes strain through the feeble gray light, searching the snow covered horizon. Great crystals of snow fall in a relentless avalanche of silence while I slowly become aware of approaching doom just beyond my senses...and then I'm carried away. With a mind hardly more than a brute animal, I cower before the fire light. With instincts that spur me to strike out and kill anything that moves, yet I sit in awe and envy of the birdlike dancing shaman across the blazing embers. It is he that knows, it is he that can show me, it is he alone that can strike fear into my brutal soul. And now I sit in a high window encircled with fragrant honeysuckles. The birds of the glen announce the morning of spring, and a chalk-white mare grazes off there in the meadow below while I try to capture this memory to carry with me on my journey to Jerusalem, for I fear I may fall beneath the sword of the infidel Saracen and return no more. Now I see the burning heat and the loneliness. In the midst of this desert and solitude, I am assured of the nearness of God—Antioch is taken! The mountains are white and molten in the late October sun. The wind rises and I'm swept away along with it. I am crushed with noise; noise that reaches the sky, noise that shakes the very earth itself. The air is acrid with the stench of chemicals and the density of human habitation. The ground is hard, hot, filthy pavement. I see the slums and squalor, crevices packed with the accumulated filth of generations. Pain, frustration, loathing, hatred, fear, crime, negation, death and despair. The victors have become the victims. Self-inflicted afflictions. Suicide, insanity, a vision of hell pounds at my senses like storm breakers against a sea wall. Hideousness and revulsion flood my being...but this time, I am not carried away. It is the ultimate evil, a force of evil which denies the spirit and laughs at Honor. Only the ultimate dream can defeat the ultimate nightmare. Here is the last test of manhood, here is the battle compared to which all others were but jest. Here is where we stand as Men or die like dogs. God grant the Oak will stand. God grant the Ravens will think and remember our names among the brave and noble who held back the FOE. God grant we quit ourselves like men. God grant.

—Dolph 1967

Well, are you about to puke? Or maybe you're saying, "Yeah, I know where you're coming from!" It may not be good poetry, but it clearly says where I was in those last years before I met my Mentor and before my baptism and initiation process began. It wreaks of youthful idealism, but it also illustrates the power and presence of archetypal language, I was trying to "Speak the Bones" to myself. So much of the symbolism and many of the principles that show up in these "poems" anticipated and mirrored concepts encompassed by the initiation Tradition. In my own case, even the vocabulary fit the cultural derivation and context. Yes, I was something of a prodigy, but the important thing is to see the immature idealism in the uninitiated male. There's an old saying, "In every man there's a poet who died young." Poets don't die of old age! They wither away due to frustration and a lack of room to grow and mature. Youthful idealism and romanticism, properly cultivated through initiation, grows into True Maturity, unshakeable principle, True Masculine Character, nobility of spirit and, above all a satisfaction in life that's worth more than all the money, power, psychiatric therapy, good looks, good health, whatever, whatever!

This last set of writings, "poems" if you will, are selected examples which illustrate changes in my character and outlook during the past twenty to thirty years. I hope they reveal maturity…not just advancing old age…and that my youthful idealism has been preserved; the "poet" didn't die, but was nurtured, preserved and refined. Nor am I an aging adolescent. I have married, fathered five children, and am Grandfather to sixteen (!) Grandchildren, I've been employed in the same profession for eighteen years, my credit rating is excellent, I have a few close friends, enjoy the esteem of my co-workers, seem to be thought "wise" and witty by those who know me, am often sought out for advice, asked my opinion on a wide variety of subjects and seem to have the respect that every man hopes to have at my age. From a purely subjective view, I am enormously happy! My tastes, needs and wants are simple and few. Quite frankly, I can't imagine how I came to be so fortunate in life. Have I had any problems over the years? You betcha! Lots of them...big ones! But, they don't get you down when you know who you are, where you came from and where you need to go. The wisdom, the insights, the understanding, the "Tricks of the Trade" see you through. I won't bore you with the string of absolutely astounding MIRACLES that have accompanied me on my course in life. Did I deserve them, am I saintly, am I all that "good"? No, but I chalk it up to the old saying, "The Lord takes care of fools and dogs." That seems to apply to Tricksters and Lost Dogs, as well!

Some may think I'm proposing a substitute for Christianity or some entirely "new" religion. All I can really say is...if you think I'm describing a "religion", then you really don't know much about religion! What then, am I saying that God favors male initiation? I suppose so, in the same sense that God favors any kind of proper, useful EDUCATION.

I'll leave it at that. Now, let's move on to these last examples of poetic utterance.

◆   ◆   ◆

THE RAVEN'S SONG

The Raven is a bird without a song, just a prosaic, raucous croak. He's the symbol of memory and original thought. He is the bird of solitude and reflection; a bit sad but not cynical. It is the Raven's lot in life to cleanse the world of that which is dead and decaying. The Raven cannot sing for himself, so we and all of Creation, must sing for him. The Raven's song is the inexplicable thrill that comes with the first sign of Autumn; the cold rains and dreary days. It is the indefinable stirrings we experience when watching a flight of wild geese or hear that one last cricket in the grass. It's the feeling that trees sigh in sorrow for those who cannot hear the message of cosmic meaning they wish to convey. It is those moments when we look up at billowing clouds and are struck by a strange far-away urge that can neither be described or expressed, and we can only whisper, "What is it?" What it is—is the Raven's sweet song. When we glance across a field of wild grasses in late fall or winter, we see only grays and browns, but look again…study it. There are subtle shades of yellow, rose, lavender, gold and purple. A wealth of tapestry textures in the varieties of grasses and wild plants. It is that unexpected sense of knowing and communing, yet not always knowing exactly what it is you know. That's the Raven's song. Perhaps it is the sudden welling-up of awareness that we too are a child of Nature; that our true home on this earth is the Wilderness with all the exaltation of knowing our true purpose and identity. Then it is that we must sing the Raven's song. Then it is that all of Nature sings the Raven's song. And the Raven's song sings us.

—Dolph 1991

THE RAIDERS OF AUTUMN

The harvest is in and the peasant is fat and content. While he folds his hands in slumber before a winter's fire, we cry the Hunt and ride with the rushing wind upon the Golden quest. Oak leaves and acorns, pine cones and cat tails, maple leaves on fire with the passion of autumn, a'blush with the kiss of frost. A golden treasury free for the taking. Let us go a'Viking, wild rovers of the woods, ranging far to plunder Gaia's jewel box. Apples of autumn we'll leave for the stay-at-homes, it's

Raven's bread we'll wrest from the Oak. Let us go wending, hunting horns a'blare. Our bows are bent, our spears poised in the hunt for the masterfully wrought gold of autumn, the treasures of the Lord. Wild Raiders are we, humbly stealing what's already bequeathed us. Pity the slow-witted yard dog who never thinks to passionately embrace what is his; would never take by main what is offered him. Pity those who have only goods to show, when they might have harvested memories. Cast away mere merchandise and gather a dream. Let the dullard make slaves of barley, we'll stalk the wild bee to his mead honey home. The winking Raven will lead us to old Loki's own den, where we'll tweak his pointy beard and laugh at his stunned surprise. Never confuse comfort with liberty, take company with the Brothers of the Hunt, while we ride in wild pursuit of the red and gold leaves of autumn that fly upon the breath of God. What Honor can there be in a life of hesitation? What joy can there be in waiting? The world is grand and wide when viewed from the Raven's tor. AUF DER JAGD!

THE LORDS AND THEIR SWORDS

The Lords must have their swords
With such they feed the raven
But the Raven shows the way
To the Loyal Huntsman's prey
Thus he says by deeds
What he never would in words
(a snide aside)

—Dolph 1995

MISERICORDE

Beware the Grey Man; I know dangerous things. Blood, fire, storm and stone. Heed my advice to stand in awe of the spire, respect the city gate. Step aside for the ploughman, but spit upon your whetstone and grind a fine edge to your blade for the followers of the god-who-limps. Only the Great Lord of the forests deep and mountains high shall you love. Take his servants for your friends and companions. The Raven is your rightful brother; great requiem bird of myth and legend, master of irony, lord of wintry fields. Bear the sword of justice with reluctance, it is too great for thee. It tugs heavily upon the body, it binds hard upon the belly, squeezing out the bile of ambition, in turn pressing upon the heart. Take yet the dagger, the broad ox-tongue of the Hunt, the instrument of mercy, the misericorde. Far better to deliver the coup de grace than to deal out the stroke of justice. The dagger is light and nimble, a handsome weapon that we may ill afford to be without. Thou canst wield it always in good conscience, nay, but canst wield it moreover with nobility and unimpeachable Honor. Justice is a grave and ungainly burden, handle it only when thou must, then handle it right well. Prefer instead the exercise of the dagger and never let your ambition reach further than its length. Remember, every forest is enchanted, but every castle is haunted.

—Dolph 1996

THE LORD OF WINTRY FIELDS

Although much maligned and often overlooked, the raven is the quint-essential bird of the High Middle Ages. Far more than the owl, the eagle or even the falcon. The raven plays a role in more stories and events than any other bird. He is the great requiem bird of myth and legend, master of irony, lord of wintry fields, little brother of the Hunt. The raven was often the central character, or at least a prime instrument, in many medieval folk tales. The Raven is the personification of the Trickster archetype, the manipulator of things and events; the instructor, messenger, bearer of wisdom. Pliny the Elder noted that the raven "is the only bird which seems to understand what it augurs." Of course the Norse god, Odin, would have been a complete nobody without Huginn and Munnin, his two ravens, upon whom he depended for information about what was going on in the world. We should recall that Father Noah first sent a raven in search of land. The Raven, true to his "Love a good joke!" nature, never returned; leaving Father Noah to wonder if he had found land or had simply drowned. (Of course we know he found land, otherwise there would be no ravens today). And it was also ravens which God sent to feed the Prophet Elijah in the desert. There were many so-called "Raven Saints" during the Middle Ages. One of my favorites is the Blessed St. Meinrad, martyred in 861 AD. They were all associated in some way with ravens, either they kept them as pets, were followed by ravens, their dead bodies were guarded by ravens, or some other notable detail. People of the Middle Ages believed that in the Garden of Eden, ravens had rainbow colored plumage. Modern ornithologists have found that the raven is biologically related to the so-called "birds of Paradise" and is thus classified among those rainbow birds. Medieval peoples also believed that in Paradise the Raven sang the sweetest song of all the birds. Strangely enough, ornithologists also classify the raven as a song bird! Ravens are now known to be by far the most intelligent of all the birds, many have found them to be far more intelligent than dogs. Ravens can learn human language and have been observed teaching words to their young. Astoundingly, ravens actually UNDERSTAND language and aren't simply "parroting" what they hear. And scientists have confirmed the old Hunters' tale that ravens actually do understand what a man with weapons is up to and will deliberately lead him to game, knowing that the gut-pile will be his reward. The Raven is a living link to that mystical age of chivalry.

—Dolph 1995

PAYING THE PIPER

As you may know, Grimm's Fairy Tales aren't just entertainment, they are social commentary, an instruction manual for children and adults alike. But while most of us know the story of the Pied Piper, who among us really understands its message?

In brief, it's a tale about the medieval city of Hamelin in Germany. It was a leading city of the Hanseatic League, ruled by rich and greedy merchants. According to the story, Hamelin was infested by rats, and the city fathers were at their wits end; there seemed to be no way to rid the city of this vermin.

Perhaps these "rats" were symbolic of some unwanted element of the city of Hamelin…criminals, beggars, foreign competitors…or perhaps they were simply RATS which ate up their food, destroyed their property and infected them with the dreaded Black Plague. In any case, rats served the purpose of demonstrating who the real "rats" in Hamelin were…the city fathers, themselves.

One day, a Pied Piper came to town. He was called "pied" meaning "multi-colored", in reference to his rainbow colored garb. Now right off, you and I know he was a Raven (a Trickster). You will also note, if you care to read the story again, that the Piper is never referred to as a man. In reality, the Pied Piper is a character trait, a force of nature, a mechanism whereby the city fathers are to learn a hard lesson. The Trickster is a teacher, sometimes he teaches object lessons. A valuable ally, but also the Master of Just Desserts! But even at his worst, he always tries to give his opponent the chance to learn the lesson and mend his ways.

So, as the story goes, the Piper plays his pipes and all the rats follow him down to the banks of the river Weser, jump in and drown. When the Piper returns to collect his thousand guilders, the city fathers reduce it to fifty guilders! (Seeing the rats are all gone for good, they want to avoid keeping their word.) So, the Piper plays again; this time leading all the children of Hamelin away, never to be seen again.

The moral of the story is simple and straightforward: Those who value money above Honor are doomed to lose their children! No amount of money or pleading will bring them back. And any Pied Piper can draw them away, never to return.

—Dolph 1995

PENUMBRA

PENUMBRA! Place between sleeping and waking, moment when the flow of breath moves from one nostril to the other, place between twilight and dawn, moment of solstice and equinox

...the Way Between Worlds.

PENUMBRA! Cat's eye, boast of sheela na gig, maiden's prize, portal of motherhood, siren's snare, mystery of the rose, door of life, door of ecstasy, beckoning

...the Way Between Worlds.

PENUMBRA! Serpent's eye, fish of sand, signature of the Apostles' Faith, cathedral door, dragon ship between sea and sky, two lines of standing stones tracing the Viking's grave, marking

...the Way Between Worlds.

PENUMBRA! Silence plays between the tones of the harp, in rest is music as much as the plucking of strings, the ethereal edge dividing the note and silence, singing of

...the Way Between Worlds.

PENUMBRA! Threshold of the senses, corpus callosum, keltic knot-work of nerves, braided causeway between tedious pragmatism and ever-new delights, highroad on

> ...the Way Between Worlds.

PENUMBRA! Borderland of realities, as the eye is the window of the soul, rainbow bridge of Valhalla myth, thin edge of light, heimdal guard it well, let the hansard never tread

> ...the Way Between Worlds.

PENUMBRA! Circle of light overtaking the realm of darkness, in that eclipse a door, the double circle, one complete, one broken, spilling into the world, times collide, opening

> ...the Way Between Worlds.

PENUMBRA! Mandorla, iron bands of the grail well, where the child first meets death, the boy the father, the young man Honor, the Old Man peace, and the one-eyed man sees

> ...the Way Between Worlds.

PENUMBRA! Dagger's slender blade, slithery and subtle, mercy's sting, raven perches and turns on the bright edge, flutters and croaks, showing

> ...the Way Between Worlds.

PENUMBRA! Ox-tongue, weapon of death, instrument of mercy, misericorde, the coup de grace, most noble weapon of all, easing

...the Way Between Worlds.

PENUMBRA! Rites of the Honored dead, blood of the living, tradition that merges past with present, ancestors touched, the cycle completed, the eternal return, mending

...the Way Between Worlds.

PENUMBRA! Initiate's wound, straw death, vows of Honor setting him against the hordes of trollheim, the darkman, grendl's kin, death taken hostage to serve as unwilling ally along

...the Way Between Worlds.

PENUMBRA! Dagger's edge, sword bridge of sangreal, where every warrior must pass to attain the quest, narrow way, no place to halt, no turning back from

...the Way Between Worlds.

PENUMBRA! The hanged man smiles, the lost king sighs, the coward quakes, the Raven laughs, the young find purpose, the Old find meaning, the ignorant scoff, the wicked scheme, but all seek

...the Way Between Worlds.

—Dolph 1993

THE COURT OF THE ROSE

An inspiration received at sunset Thursday, May 25, 1995. A Rite of Reconciliation. A Statement of Recognition and Respect. No True Man can speak ill of the Sisters, and no True Sister can turn away from the Loyal Huntsman.

The Court of the Rose; from which The Sacred Sisters speak Ex Cathedra. Three times three, they are the Maiden, Mother and Matriarch. They are the Rose...beauty, purity, sacrifice. The three wounds of the Rose are these...loss of innocence, child bearing, the course of the moon. They are the Pleiades; the sweet influence to constrain and inspire. They are the red of the Rose to the black of the Raven. They are the mother of swans. In the House of Swans the Hunter learns civility. In return, the Court of the Rose may claim service and protection of the Lord of Wintry Fields. The rites and wisdom of the Sisters prevail in spring time and summer, in contradistinction to the Huntsmen who, like Orion, arise in autumn and winter. The Sisters are worthy to claim the Raven's track, the rune of protection. They are the receptacle of new life, those who tend the bounty of the land, keepers of the Heimat. The Sisters instruct the Huntsman in matters of courtesy and conduct, as the Order trains and warrants the Brothers in the virtues of True Manhood. It is the duty and right of the Court of the Rose to speak against the unjust, the wicked, perverse and unruly. It is their duty to shame them, denounce them, to mock them, to deny them all comfort and consolation until they make amends. The Court of the Rose and the Order of the Death bond mirror one another, yet not as opposites, but as complementaries, each of the other. They are counterparts in the tasks, duties and rewards of life. Yet their rites are their own and a mystery to the Brothers. The bond of the red and the black is acknowledged and reaffirmed at the vernal equinox when the Brothers bring flowers to the Sisterhood at the Honor Stone. In like manner, the scepter is passed again to the Brotherhood at the autumnal equinox when the Sisters come to the Stone bearing a basket of acorns for the Huntsmen.

The formal presentation of this rite of reconciliation by the Brotherhood naturally and effectively invokes the implicit approval and binding support of the Order in its entirety, and of all Men of Honor everywhere. It remains for the Court of the Rose to formulate a statement of equal recognition and respect toward the Brotherhood, and to define the proper presentation thereof. (NOTE: The "Rose" serves also as an acronym for Rights of Social Expectation).

OH, FOR THE LIFE OF A HUNTSMAN!

While hunting was enormously popular in the Middle Ages, it was generally conducted only in groups...LARGE groups! These were very formal, even ritualized events, and might involve the entire household or court.

Among the lower classes, a hunt might consist of a more informal outing, but certainly with no less than two or three men and their dogs. The Solitary Hunter was a rare phenomenon; after all, the forests were populated by strange and fabulous beasts, spirits of earth, air, fire and water, the souls of the restless dead, the elder spirits, pagan gods, demons and wild men. All in all, not a proper place for a Christian man alone, surely a lone figure entering the woods must have special powers to commune with, or to control these dark forces. Only the outcasts of society were at home in the forests: madmen, wizards, hermits and outlaws...and a fifth; the Huntsman.

Even the dull-witted could sense the almost palpable force that sprang up like a wall at the forest's edge. The Huntsman must then be a somewhat mystical being himself. It was well known that wild ravens led Huntsmen to their quarry. Who knew what other communications took place between man and bird! Surely these Ravens taught him other secret and magical wisdom as well.

But let us define our terms; any fool with weapons could call himself a hunter, but a Huntsman was a professional who gained his livelihood from the Hunt. He was as skilled and respected in his craft as any modern scholar, physician or other authority figure. The Medieval Huntsman is most often remembered today as a standard character in faery tales. It was the Loyal Huntsman who was ordered to take Snow-white into the forest and murder her. But it was the Huntsman's high moral virtue that saved her life instead. Such natural nobility was a defining trait in the depiction of the Huntsman in folk tales of the time. In real life, the Huntsman was essential to the well-being of every household. A company of Huntsmen were attached to every royal personage, manor and community. His duties were not confined to simply keeping everyone well fed. Huntsmen acted as scouts, spies, couriers, map makers, advisors, ambassadors...and assassins!

A warranted Huntsman was in a unique position to serve in these many capacities. While it is not commonly understood today, in ancient times, virtually all societies existed as police states and, unlike other commoners, the Huntsman could move freely without arousing the least suspicion. The Huntsman might be found at any hour of the day or night on the highways and byways, in the taverns and market places, in the stables or kitchens, fully armed and mingling with whomsoever he pleased. Prince and peasant alike delighted in the company of these free-ranging High-steppers; they were boon companions and welcome wherever they went.

The Huntsman enjoyed a kind of social equality with the nobility precisely because they shared the same interests and experiences. The nobleman was always eager to curry favor with the Huntsman because of his position as a master of the Hunt; to be his friend was to be presumed a good hunter oneself, and in this matter, the Huntsman was the First among Equals.

Furthermore, the Huntsman could always be relied upon to provide news and gossip, tales of far places and marvelous events. In return he would naturally hear such gossip, stories and bits of information as the stay-at-home might have to offer. While every Huntsman was a potential spy, this fact was tacitly ignored because the Huntsman was held in such high esteem and so universally liked. His friendship was so highly valued that to suspect him of spying was to deny oneself the pleasure of his company...and perhaps to imply that one had something to hide!

The Huntsman of the High Middle Ages (and most other times and places for that matter) stood alone as the most revered and valued common man. The Huntsman enjoyed greater personal liberty than any other...more freedom even than their highborn masters. The Hunt, the Quest, the Pilgrimage, they are all one. Oh, for the life of the Huntsman!

THE RIVER ETERNAL

It's the riverbed that shapes, guides and defines the water. The water today isn't the water yesterday and won't be the water of tomorrow. But the river is the same because the riverbed is the same. It's the bed that's so important. We don't see the bed, we have to think about it to know it's there. But without the bed, the water would just spread aimlessly across the land, becoming shallow and weak; it would just sink into the earth or dry up and disappear in the sun's heat. It's the bed that guides the water on, directing it back to the Great Sea from which it came. When the water is gone, then you can see the bed. Then the riverbed is all there is to see. It tells us little about the great rushing tide, the noise and tumult, the power and animation of the water itself. The river without water is mere archaeology; dry stones, dull history, a Babylonian brick-pile with no life to interpret the once living flow of humanity. That's what the River Eternal is...people. religion, meaning, culture, breath, eating, sleeping, laughing, talking...and place. That place is the context; the riverbed. People flow along its course. Our ancestors carved out that place; the surest path for us to follow, and we do well to stay within its banks. Not because it's safe, but because we best fulfill our purpose and attain the true desires of our hearts. It's the nature of water to dig away at the stream banks, always seeking a quicker, easier, newer course. Sometimes a new and better course is found. Sometimes a new and better direction is set and the flow of one or many lives is changed forever. But too often the eaten-away bank collapses, blocking the water's retreat and leaving a mere eddy, a back-water, a stagnant pool. At times the stream narrows and the water rushes on in a torrent. At other times the banks are wide allowing the waters to drift lazily, creating many cross currents. But always moving inexorable toward the Great Sea beyond. We are the People, we are the water. Without the guiding disciplines of religion, tradition, culture and place we are a great stagnant swamp. But with the sturdy constraints of a well-defined channel, we are powerful and meaningful. We are energized and directed. We turn fate into destiny and flow on to meet and merge with it.

For my daughter, Erin. Oct. 28, 1993

ON BEING A REAL MAN

When I was a kid in school, I recall being faced with a math exam that I hadn't studied for. I was wishing for a miracle; maybe God could just zap the answers into my head so I could pass. You know what? He didn't! Some things you just have to work for. In the same way, God could just zap wisdom and character into us when we turn twenty-one, but He doesn't. What's more, he won't! Character, by definition, is one of those things you have to earn. It's like genuine respect; you can't demand it, you have to work for it. We're all born male, but we have to LEARN to be a Man.

The Hunting Orders offer a series of initiations and training that move the candidate through the various stages of life-experience. This process insures that the candidate accomplishes the required psychological growth and maturity in a greatly accelerated manner. All the issues of life can be confronted, resolved and assimilated. The last and greatest issue of life, one's own mortality, is also faced. The fear of death, the regrets of life's mistakes, the resentments of lost opportunities and all unfinished business are resolved...joyfully. In a very real sense, death itself is taken hostage and forced to play a constructive role in one's life. The initiation process can show you the meaning of life and give you a distinct purpose in life. The process can prepare you to deal effectively and objectively with every aspect of life without becoming bogged down in the usual emotional confusion and difficulties.

The initiation process is something we must all face anyway, it's just a question of whether we will do it in a formal, deliberate way that assures a high degree of success or face it piecemeal, accidentally and spread out at random during the course of a lifetime...and perhaps in circumstances and moments when we are least prepared to meet them.

What you'll experience and learn is far different and far more profound than you imagine. And if you have a son, a grandson, a nephew, if you have a friend, a co-worker, neighbor, even a neighbor's child...and yes, daughters too...you're a role model, whether you want to be or not. If you care about any of these people, if you care about yourself and your own future, you have an obligation to exhibit the character of True Manhood. Where possible, you should try to be a mentor to these people. The ultimate proof of real Manhood is the desire and ability to point the way to Manhood (Adulthood) for others.

Humanity is so much dust. A circle drawn in the dust marks our place, our culture, our individual lives. Without the dust no circle can be drawn. Without the circle, we are only dust...and the Ages pass us by unnoticed. We are obliged by our very nature to draw a circle if we can. The Orden der Valknut is the instrument whereby a circle is drawn that cuts deep and is not soon blown away by the winds of time.

Our people, culture and nation are going to hell—literally! Crooks in government and gangs in the streets. What can you, one man, do? You can work on yourself first. You can hold others to standards of excellence. And you can sponsor at least one other lost dog. If each and every one of us did that, we could turn this country around in a year.

Although I like to try, there is really nothing I can say to convince you how important this opportunity really is for every man. It's something that we must each, individually commit to and experience on a gut-level to attain. I hope you'll follow through. You may not have another chance.

Western Civilization, and America especially, puts a lot of pressure on males to "prove their manhood", but offers virtually no incentive to do so, nor any valid standard by which to measure the results. Our culture is permeated by moral cowardice; cynical, corrupt weaklings who struggle to get by on compromise. Our Nation is populated by "pretend people"; those with no real life. They are not real people…they simply don't have the guts to become REAL people. You know the throw-away expression… "Get a life"? Well, here's your chance! Thank you for your time and attention.

—Dolph, October 28, 2000

Declaration of Auspices

We, the undersigned, as Loyal Huntsmen, Brotherhood of Sicarii, Orden der Valknut, do here declare our regret for the publication of this knowledge which, since the founding of our Order, has been held privileged. However, we also recognize the great need to preserve this very knowledge and to hand it down to future generations intact and uncorrupted. We speak specifically of Part Two: "Traditions of the Hunt", in this present work, entitled, "BOOK of the HUNT". We have reviewed this part and approve, endorse and recommend it as accurate and correct. We have also conferred among ourselves regarding the formulation and adoption of the "Origination Ceremony" for the spontaneous creation of freeborn Guilds and Lodges of our Hunting Order. We find the Ceremony both worthy and effective. We hereby endorse its adoption and use as a permanent part of our Tradition. No other parts of this present work have been reviewed and no endorsement by our Order is implied or intended. While we may privately approve of it, in principle it must be considered by us as the personal experiences and remembrances of the author and we must, therefore, withhold all judgment and allow it to stand upon its own merit.

Signed in company and mutual witness upon the Feast Day of Saint Hubert of Liege, this third day of November, in the year of Our Lord, Two Thousand.

_____   _____
Henry Travis Cosgrove, LH   Alfred Kent Scifres, LH

The Reading List

I could recommend a hundred important books relevant to this subject, you wouldn't read them. I will limit recommended reading to those I feel are at the very TOP of such a list.

The <u>HOLY BIBLE</u>. Any valid translation. This isn't a token recommendation, if you haven't read it, you don't know what it says...and you certainly don't know what it says about the subject at hand.

<u>WILDMEN, WARRIORS and KINGS, Masculine Spirituality and the Bible</u>. By Patrick M. Arnold. 1991. Crossroad Publishing.

<u>FORESTS, The Shadow of Civilization</u>. By Robert Pogue Harrison. 1992. University of Chicago Press.

<u>IRON JOHN</u>. By Robert Bly. 1990. Addison-Wesley Publishing Co.

<u>BEYOND THE HERO</u>. Allan B. Chinen, MD. 1993. Tarcher-Putnam.

<u>IN DEFENSE OF HUNTING</u>. James A. Swan. 1995. Harper Collins.

<u>ORION'S LEGACY</u>. Charles Bergman. 1996. Dutton.

And from the Ladies: <u>A RETURN TO MODESTY, Discovering the Lost Virtues</u>. Wendy Shalit. 1999. The Free Press.

Important Notice

Upon further reflection and a final consultation, the decision has been taken to <u>NOT</u> publish the illustrations in this text. Those illustrations are available upon request via the Internet. This will establish individual, "One on one" contact, provide more appropriate authorization, and more direct assistance to those willing to act as Originators of new chapters.

There is no charge for this service.

To request the illustrations, for other information and assistance, you may contact the Brotherhood at one of the e-mail addresses listed below. In addition, you will be directed to our website and weekly newsletter.

honorstone@yahoo.com

honorstone@hotmail.com

honorstone@lycos.com

honorstone@netscape.net

-or-

tomdolph@yahoo.com

Addendum

As it happens, the Altmann who presided at my own Third Initiation has now reviewed this manuscript and commented. In response to those comments, and relevant to matters raised since then, I will add information regarding the following four topics and a fifth.

1. I have deliberately neglected to discuss **the Naming Ceremony**. Fraternal names are seldom used and often disliked (I didn't like mine!).

2. "**The Mark**" designates a geographic area or matter over which a Huntsman has final authority. Any animal taken within bow shot of where the Huntsman stands at the moment of the kill is under his jurisdiction. Any matter that takes place within a three day march of his customary place of residence is under his jurisdiction. This matter can become complicated, thus I have chosen not to discuss it. This also involves the Landrecht: common law. That which is right, upright, just, true, fair, real, suitable, proper. Those rules, principles, conventional wisdom and standards which are commonly understood among Men of Honor as being the Law of God and Nature.

3. **The Toggle**. A spike (no more than three inches long) from the antlers of a deer or elk attached to a hunting spear, just behind the blade. This serves to prevent an impaled boar from rushing the length of the spear shaft and wounding the Hunter before it dies. The Toggle is used especially in hunting wild boar, which historically has symbolized satan and the anti-Christ. Antler has always been a symbol of The Hunt, manhood, virility and spiritual strength, as in "The horn (strength) of my Salvation". Worn on a black cord around one's neck as a

choker (horizontally with the point toward the right and the base inscribed with the "LH" bind rune, which is also identical to the Chi-Rho symbol), the Toggle symbolizes our protection by God against the power of satan and the antiChrist.

4. **The Hantsel Days**. The five days left over from the 360 Prophetic days of the year. These days are observed at various times by different cultures and groups within cultures. Our Order observes the five days beginning October 29th, the anniversary of the Audita Tremendi, through November 2nd; November 3rd being the Feast of Saint Hubert. During these five days, all members of the Order, as Men of Honor, are to reflect on all promises made by them during the past year, and to make good their word, however casual or trivial the matter may have been. All promises, bargains, debts and agreements must be finalized. All borrowed items must be returned in good order or replaced. All declarations and vows completed, all grievances resolved. It is the DUTY of all Men of Honor to remind their Brothers of any forgotten matter so that it can be resolved honorably.

5. **Funeral Rite**. Four branches of Oak (in spring or summer) or Pine (in fall or winter) are to be placed around the site where the Huntsman (or his ashes) is to be buried; north, south, east and west. The eldest Brother stands at the west end of the site holding the deceased's hunting spear. The butt of the spear rests on the earth, the blade pointing to the Heavens indicating the direction his soul has flown. When the Priest or Minister has concluded Christian rites for the dead, each Huntsman present will place an acorn or pine cone on the grave and depart. Last of all, the Eldest Huntsman will place a wreath of oak leaves or pine bows on the burial site, take up the spear and depart.

0-595-25763-1